200
REALLY EASY RECIPES

D0993713

200

HAMLYN **ALL COLOUR COOKBOOK**

REALLY EASY
RECIPES

LOUISE PICKFORD

An Hachette UK Company
www.hachette.co.uk

First published in Great Britain in 2009 by Hamlyn,
a division of Octopus Publishing Group Ltd
Carmelite House, 50 Victoria Embankment
London EC4Y 0DZ
www.octopusbooks.co.uk

This edition published in 2016

ISBN 978-0-600-63331-0

A CIP catalogue record for this book is available from
the British Library

Printed and bound in China

10 9 8 7 6 5 4 3

Standard level spoon measurement are used in all recipes.
1 tablespoon = one 15 ml spoon
1 teaspoon = one 5 ml spoon

Both imperial and metric measurements have been given in
all recipes. Use one set of measurements only and not a
mixture of both.

Fresh herbs should be used unless otherwise stated.

Eggs should be medium unless otherwise stated. The
Department of Health advises that eggs should not be
consumed raw. This book contains dishes made with raw or
lightly cooked eggs. It is prudent for more vulnerable people
such as pregnant and nursing mothers, invalids, the elderly,
babies and young children to avoid uncooked or lightly
cooked dishes made with eggs. Once prepared these dishes
should be kept refrigerated and used promptly.

Ovens should be preheated to the specific temperature – if
using a fan-assisted oven, follow manufacturer's instructions
for adjusting the time and the temperature.

This book includes dishes made with nuts and nut
derivatives. It is advisable for customers with known
allergic reactions to nuts and nut derivatives to check
the labels of pre-prepared ingredients for the possible
inclusion of nut derivatives.

contents

introduction

introduction

This book is the perfect choice for first-time cooks. It offers a wonderful collection of simple-to-prepare dishes guaranteed to make every mealtime easy. Featuring a winning combination of all-time favourites, classics with a new twist as well as some new and exciting dishes, all the recipes have easy-to-follow methods using ingredients readily available from your local supermarket, making shopping a breeze.

Variety is the spice of life, and with so many meal ideas on offer here, you'll never be short of choice. Dishes range from tempting breakfast and brunch ideas and satisfying pasta, rice and noodle dishes to time-saving one-pot meals (with very little washing-up) and wickedly decadent puddings. So there's something here to tempt even the most reticent cook!

Cooking is all about confidence, and the more you cook and familiarize yourself with the equipment, ingredients and cooking methods, the easier and more enjoyable it becomes. It won't be long before you're cooking for yourself and your friends, and showing off your newfound culinary confidence!

the feel-good factor

If you're leaving home for the first time and/or starting college or a job, the experience can be rather daunting and demanding, and providing yourself and your friends with good food can seem like an extra, unwanted chore. Of course, there are many fast-food options available, but although convenient, they are often expensive and in many cases high in fat and lacking in nutritional value. If you're studying or working hard in a new job, you'll need plenty of energy to help concentration levels, so eating well is especially important, not to mention comforting! Cooking from scratch means that you have control over exactly what you eat, so you can avoid those hidden ingredients in take-away and convenience foods that offer 'empty' calories. Instead, you can opt for a balanced diet with lean meat and fish for protein, carbohydrates for fuel and fresh fruit and vegetables for the essential vitamins and fibre that will keep your body's systems running smoothly. This book will provide you with nutritious as well as delicious dishes to

give you an overall sense of well-being when you need it most as well as optimum energy.

This is also a time when being in the kitchen means less time to socialize with friends and relax, so most of the dishes in this book are quick to prepare and cook – even those that are fit for a special occasion.

Just as important, however, is the satisfaction you will gain from mastering a new skill – eating well to live well!

about the recipes

The recipes are divided into seven chapters so choosing just the right dish for every occasion a simple and speedy process.

Breakfast is the most important meal of the day and one that often consists only of a quick caffeine fix, but this energy hit is short-lived. The range of dishes in Breakfasts & Brunch will ensure that you have something great to eat everyday. Whether it's a healthy Summer Berry Granola, Bacon & Maple Syrup Pancakes or the hearty Rösti with Ham & Eggs, you can get your morning off to the perfect start.

Soups & One-pot Meals provides valuable time-saving options and recipes that are also a godsend for those with a limited supply of utensils. Many recipes in this chapter make warming winter dishes, such as Beef Goulash and Chilli Bean & Red Pepper Soup, when you need something more substantial to get you through chilly evenings and provide you with the necessary fuel for the following day. Leftovers can be frozen for another day, or those from other dishes such as Chicken & Rice Bake can be stored in plastic containers for satisfying packed lunches.

Working hard and playing hard often leaves little time and energy for cooking, but don't worry because 20-minute Suppers has the answer – great meals in moments. Choose from a spicy Thai Chicken Curry, Italian-inspired Tuna & Pesto Burgers or the sophisticated Lamb with Olive & Pine Nut Salsa. All the recipes in this chapter make ideal dinner party dishes, so why not impress friends and family with these sure-fire meals?

If you're studying hard at college or university, or you've begun a new job for the first time, you'll need plenty of energy, so a chapter packed full of carbohydrate-based dishes such as those you'll find in Pasta, Rice & Noodles will hit the spot. Fuel up on Sausage Meatballs, Peas & Pasta, Baked Risotto with Burnt Butter or a simple Pad Thai noodle dish.

Meat and fish are relatively expensive, but in order to maintain a healthy diet, it's essential to eat protein when we can. There are plenty of dishes in Meat, Poultry & Fish that use cheaper cuts of meat, such as minced beef and lamb, chicken wings and ribs. And although most fish are pricey, they are definitely worth reserving for a special occasion or a dinner party. You can also substitute cheaper kinds of fish in most of the recipes.

Vegetarian Dishes & Salads is perfect for all non meat-eaters, although there are many more meat-free dishes dotted throughout the book offering a wide variety of delicious meals. Try the Moroccan-inspired Chickpea Tagine, the aromatic Mixed Vegetable Curry or the fancy Halloumi & Fig Pastry Pizza.

The final chapter Easy Puds & Cakes is for those with a sweet tooth, packed full of sumptuous desserts and sweets treats for everyday as well as for entertaining. Chocolate Refrigerator Cake, for example, serves up to 30 people and keeps well, making it a perfect mid-morning snack to go with coffee. There is a lovely Fruit Salad with Elderflower Syrup for the summer months, while the Sticky Toffee Puddings are ideal for winter.

storecupboard essentials

Keeping a well-stocked store cupboard is both useful and great for last minute suppers. Here are a few essential items...

Extra virgin olive oil and vegetable oil These are essential for salad dressings as well as for frying and roasting.

White wine vinegar, red wine vinegar and balsamic vinegar These are good options for both marinating meat and poultry for more tender results and for piquant salad dressings.

Canned chopped tomatoes A must for making flavourful sauces for all kinds of dishes.

Canned tuna in olive oil It is both healthy and tasty, and can be used either cold in salads or as a spread, or served hot in a pasta sauce or made into fish cakes.

Canned chickpeas and red kidney beans
These are great for making quick salads and
also for adding to soups, stews and casseroles.
Dried pasta and noodles They are endlessly
versatile, for using cold to make salads as well
as for hot main meals and adding to soups.
Keep a selection of different forms, such as
spaghetti, penne and fusilli pasta and rice
noodles and thread and medium egg noodles.
Spices and dried herbs These can be
accumulated gradually, a different one each
week, to build up a versatile selection, including
ground cumin, coriander and turmeric, jerk
seasoning and dried chilli flakes for adding
aromatic flavour and heat; ground cinnamon for
both sweet and savoury dishes; dried oregano
and thyme for Mediterranean flavouring.
Sea salt and whole black peppercorns These
are the best options for everyday seasoning, to
grind fresh for maximum flavour.
Basmati, long-grain and risotto rice Rice adds
bulk to a meal, and also makes delicious meals
in its own right, such as pilafs and risottos.
Plain and self-raising flours These are vital for
baking and for making cheese or white sauce.
**Caster sugar and soft light and dark brown
sugar** These are the most versatile sugar
options, the former being easiest to dissolve
and the latter for adding a rich flavour.
Asian sauces Sauces such as soy, oyster,
hoisin, Thai fish and sweet chilli sauce, are
great for giving stir-fry, noodle and steamed
dishes an instant flavour hit.

shopping advice
Always make a shopping list before you
shop. A weekly trip to the supermarket is
perfect for non-perishables, but if you can,
shop daily for fresh ingredients from a local
butcher, fishmonger or greengrocer as they
can help advise you on the best and cheapest
seasonal ingredients.

Although supermarkets have a fast
turnover of fresh meat and fish, always check
the 'sell by' and 'use by' dates on the labels
and only buy produce that looks fresh and
vibrant rather than tired. Butchers will often
sell you a single fillet or cut of meat, whereas
supermarkets tend to offer cheaper, bulk-
buying opportunities. With fruit and vegetables,
always look for seasonal produce, as these
will be the best quality and price. They should
feel firm, as well as appearing smooth and
wrinkle-free.

storage guidelines

Keep the more robust fruit and vegetables, such as apples, bananas, potatoes, onions and garlic, in a cool, dark place but not refrigerated. Store fresh herbs, lettuce and more delicate items in the salad drawer of your refrigerator – if you place herbs in a plastic bag with a little splash of water, they will last longer. Mushrooms are best kept in a paper or cloth bag, as they 'sweat' in plastic and spoil quickly. Store heavy items on the bottom and more delicate ones on top.

Remove meat, poultry and seafood from their plastic containers or wrappings, then wash and dry with kitchen paper and wrap them again loosely in foil. Always store fresh meat and poultry on the bottom shelf of the refrigerator so that no raw juices can drip down on to other foods, and always store cooked meat and poultry away from raw to avoid contamination.

Any fresh meat, poultry or fish you have left unused can always be frozen. Wrap in foil and place in the freezer or pack in a freezer bag. Ensure frozen food is completely thawed before cooking.

If you store eggs in the refrigerator, remember to remove 1 hour before using to return them to room temperature.

equipment checklist

Your available budget and also how much you cook will to some extent determine what cooking equipment you buy, but the following

is a recommended selection of items. This will ensure that you have everything you need for most dishes and will be a sound investment for the future, especially if you purchase good-quality cookware, which will prove much more durable.

- Selection of 3 saucepans: small, medium and large
- Large, heavy-based frying pan
- Roasting pan
- Baking sheet
- Set of scales
- 3 sharp knives: small, large and serrated-edged
- Selection of mixing bowls ranging from ramekin size to large
- Measuring jug – plastic is fine
- 2 chopping boards: one for raw foods and the other for everything else
- Large sieve
- Food processor – if you can afford it, this is a great investment and will save you a lot of time.

glossary

Chinese five spice powder An aromatic blend of spices used in Asian cooking.

Chorizo A Spanish spiced pork sausage available from the deli section of supermarkets. It has a wonderfully intense savoury flavour.

Elderflower cordial A fragrant cordial made from elderflowers and available from most supermarkets.

Frangelico A hazelnut-flavoured liqueur produced in Italy, available from larger supermarkets and wine stores or suppliers.

Halloumi cheese A ewes' or goats' milk cheese from Cyprus. It is best cooked – grilled, griddled, fried or baked – otherwise it can be chewy.

Hokkein noodles Chinese egg noodles, vacuum-packed for freshness and found in the chiller section of larger supermarkets. You can use dried as an alternative, but you will need to double up the quantity given in the recipe.

Jerk seasoning A spice mix used in Caribbean cooking, and available in the spice section of supermarkets and from specialist food stores and suppliers.

Kaffir lime leaves Another Asian ingredient, these leaves have a fantastic lime fragrance and are available from larger supermarkets, green grocers and Asian stores. Unused leaves freeze well, packed in sealed bags.

Mascarpone cheese A full-fat cream cheese used in Italian cuisine, this is especially useful in cooking, because it never curdles when heated and adds a richness to any dish.

Mirin A rice wine seasoning used in Japanese cooking, available from the Asian section of most supermarkets and health-food stores.

Pak choi Chinese greens with delicate dark green leaves and a crunchy white bulb of stalks, available all year round from supermarkets. They are high in vitamins, including A and C, as well as calcium, iron and folic acid.

Puy lentils Tiny green lentils with blue veining from France, widely available from supermarkets and health-food stores. Unlike dried beans, lentils don't need presoaking.

Star anise One of the spices used to make Chinese five spice powder, but it is also worth buying the whole spice to flavour Asian dishes.

Sumac A Middle Eastern spice, usually found in its deep red/purple ground form, with a fragrant lemon flavour. It is available from the spice section of larger supermarkets and from specialist food stores and suppliers.

Thai basil leaves A must for achieving an essential Thai flavour, but ordinary European basil will do. It is available from some supermarkets and Asian stores.

breakfasts & brunch

bacon & maple syrup pancakes

Serves **4**
Preparation time **5 minutes**
Cooking time **15 minutes**

300 g (10 oz) **plain flour**
2½ teaspoons **baking
 powder**
½ teaspoon **salt**
1 **egg**, lightly beaten
425 ml (14½ fl oz) **milk**
25 g (1 oz) **butter**, melted
spray olive oil, for oiling
8 **smoked back bacon
 rashers**
maple syrup, to serve

Sift the flour, baking powder and salt into a bowl. Make a well in the centre and gradually beat in the egg and milk. Continue to beat until the batter is smooth. Stir in the melted butter.

Heat a heavy-based frying pan until hot, spray lightly with spray oil and spoon on about 100 ml (3½ fl oz) of the pancake batter. Cook over a medium heat for 1–2 minutes until bubbles start appearing on the surface. Carefully flip the pancake over and cook for a further 1–2 minutes until browned on the underside. Remove from the pan and keep warm in a preheated oven, 150°C (300°F), Gas Mark 2, while you cook the remainder of the batter – it should make 8 pancakes in total.

Meanwhile, cook the bacon under a preheated high grill for 2 minutes on each side until golden.

Serve the pancakes topped with the bacon and drizzled with maple syrup.

For pancakes with mixed berries, prepare the pancake batter and cook the pancakes as above. Meanwhile, combine 250 g (8 oz) mixed berries with 2 tablespoons icing sugar in a saucepan and warm through over a low heat for 2–3 minutes until soft and juicy. Serve the pancakes topped with the berry sauce and some Greek yogurt.

smoked salmon scrambled eggs

Serves **1**
Preparation time **10 minutes**
Cooking time **3–4 minutes**

15 g (½ oz) **butter**
3 large **eggs**
1 tablespoon **milk**
1 tablespoon **single cream**
  (optional)
25–40 g (1–1½ oz) **smoked
  salmon**, cut into narrow
  strips
1 teaspoon finely snipped
  chives
1–2 slices of hot buttered
  toast
salt and **black pepper**

Melt the butter in a saucepan over a gentle heat until foaming.

Put the eggs in a bowl and mix well with a fork. Add the milk and season with salt and pepper.

Pour the eggs into the foaming butter and cook, stirring constantly with a wooden spoon, scraping the bottom of the pan and bringing the eggs from the outside to the centre. The eggs are done when they form soft, creamy curds and are barely set.

Remove the pan from the heat and stir in the cream, if using, salmon and chives. Pile on to the hot toast on a warmed serving plate. Serve immediately.

For scrambled eggs with goats' cheese & herbs, cook the scrambled eggs as above. Once barely set, remove the pan from the heat and stir in 100 g (3½ oz) soft goats' cheese and 2 tablespoons chopped mixed herbs. Pile on to the hot toast and serve.

rösti with ham & eggs

Serves **2**
Preparation time **10 minutes**
Cooking time **10–12 minutes**

500 g (1 lb) **waxy potatoes,**
   such as Desiree, peeled
25 g (1 oz) **butter**
2 **eggs**
2 slices of **smoked ham**
salt and **black pepper**
tomato ketchup, to serve

Grate the potatoes using a box grater and place on a clean tea towel. Wrapping them in the towel, squeeze out all the excess moisture, transfer to a bowl and season to taste with salt and pepper.

Melt the butter in a large nonstick frying pan. Divide the potato mixture into quarters and form each into a 10 cm (4 inch) cake. Add to the pan and cook over a medium heat for 5–6 minutes on each side until lightly golden.

Meanwhile, poach or fry the eggs.

Serve 2 röstis per person, topped with an egg and with a slice of smoked ham and some tomato ketchup.

For sweet potato rösti with egg & spinach, grate 250 g (8 oz) sweet potato and 250 g (8 oz) waxy potato and mix together. Make and cook the rösti as above. Serve 2 röstis topped with a poached egg and a small handful of baby spinach leaves.

asparagus with frazzled eggs

Serves **4**
Preparation time **10 minutes**
Cooking time **10 minutes**

500 g (1 lb) **asparagus
  spears**, trimmed
olive oil, for coating and
  shallow-frying
4 **eggs**, chilled
salt and **black pepper**
Parmesan shavings, to serve

Blanch the asparagus in a saucepan of salted boiling water for 2 minutes. Drain and refresh under cold water. Drain again, pat dry and toss in a little oil to coat.

Cook the asparagus in a preheated griddle pan or on a preheated barbecue for 2–3 minutes on each side until tender but still with a bite. Set aside to cool slightly.

Pour enough oil into a large frying pan to coat the base generously and heat until almost smoking. Crack each egg into a cup and carefully slide into the pan (watch out as the oil will splutter). Once the edges of the eggs have bubbled up and browned, reduce the heat to low, cover and cook for a further 1 minute. Remove from the pan with a slotted spoon and drain on kitchen paper. The yolks should have formed a skin, but should remain runny underneath.

Divide the asparagus between 4 warmed plates and top each pile with an egg. Scatter with pepper and Parmesan shavings. Serve with a little pot of salt for the eggs.

For soft-boiled eggs with asaparagus & prosciutto soldiers, blanch 20 asparagus spears as above. Drain and refresh under cold water. Drain again and pat dry. Cut 4 slices of prosciutto into 5 long, thin strips each and wrap each asparagus spear in a strip of ham. Boil 4 eggs in a saucepan of gently simmering water for 4 minutes. Transfer to egg cups, cut off the tops and serve with the ham-wrapped asparagus spears for dunking.

cheesy turkey & cranberry melt

Serves **4**
Preparation time **5 minutes**
Cooking time **8 minutes**

4 **flat rolls**
2 tablespoons **wholegrain mustard**
2 tablespoons **cranberry sauce**
200 g (7 oz) **cooked turkey breast,** sliced
125 g (4 oz) **Cheddar cheese,** grated

Split the rolls in half and spread half with the mustard and the other half with the cranberry sauce. Top with the turkey slices and cheese and sandwich together.

Heat a dry frying pan until hot, add the sandwich and cook over a medium-high heat for 4 minutes on each side until golden and the cheese has melted. Serve hot.

For avocado, blue cheese & spinach melt, split the rolls in half and spread the base of each one with a little butter. Mash together 1 peeled, stoned and sliced avocado, 50 g (2 oz) crumbled blue cheese and 2 tablespoons thick cream. Divide between the roll bases and add a few baby spinach leaves. Add the roll tops and cook as above until the filling starts to ooze.

egg & manchego tortillas

Serves **4**
Preparation time **15 minutes**,
  plus cooling
Cooking time **20 minutes**

1 **onion**, finely chopped
1 **green chilli**, deseeded and
  finely chopped, plus extra
  to serve
1 **corn on the cob**, kernels
  removed, or 4 tablespoons
  canned sweetcorn
10 **eggs**, beaten
25 g (1 oz) **butter**
75 g (3 oz) **Manchego
  cheese**, crumbled, plus
  extra shavings to serve
1 tablespoon **fresh coriander**,
  chopped, plus extra to serve
8 **flour tortillas**, warmed in
  the oven
salt and **black pepper**
snipped **chives**, to garnish
4 tablespoons **sweet chilli
  sauce**

Stir the onion, chilli and sweetcorn kernels into the beaten eggs in a bowl. Season well with salt and pepper.

Melt the butter in a large saucepan until foaming. Add the egg mixture and cook over a medium heat, stirring constantly, until the eggs are softly scrambled. Immediately remove the pan from the heat and stir in the crumbled Manchego and coriander.

Serve immediately on the warmed tortillas scattered with green chilli slices, fresh coriander and chives, plus shavings of Manchego and the sweet chilli sauce.

For homemade guacamole to serve with the tortillas in place of the sweet chilli sauce, put 1 peeled, stoned and diced avocado in a food processor or blender with 1 crushed garlic clove, 1 deseeded and chopped red chilli, juice of 1 lime, 1 tablespoon chopped fresh coriander and salt and pepper to taste. Process until fairly smooth and transfer to a bowl. Stir in 1 deseeded and finely chopped tomato.

bacon & egg crispy bread tarts

Serves **4**
Preparation time **10 minutes**
Cooking time **35 minutes**

spray olive oil, for oiling
16 slices of **white bread**
75 g (3 oz) **butter**, melted
150 g (5 oz) **smoked bacon rashers**, rind removed, diced
2 **eggs**
125 ml (4 fl oz) **double cream**
2 tablespoons freshly grated **Parmesan cheese**
8 **vine cherry tomatoes**
salt and **black pepper**

Spray a muffin tray lightly with spray oil. Cut the crusts off the bread and discard. Flatten each bread slice by rolling over it firmly with a rolling pin. Brush each slice with the melted butter and place 8 of the slices diagonally on top of the others to form the bases. Carefully press each base into a hole of the prepared muffin tray, making sure that they fit evenly (they need to reach up the sides).

Bake in a preheated oven, 200°C (400°F), Gas Mark 6, for 12–15 minutes until crisp and golden.

Meanwhile, heat a dry frying pan until hot, add the bacon and cook for 2–3 minutes until crisp and golden.

Divide the bacon between the baked bread cases. Beat together the eggs, cream, cheese and salt and pepper to taste in a bowl. Spoon into the cases and top each with a cherry tomato. Bake in the oven for 15 minutes until set.

For spinach & egg tarts, prepare and bake the bread cases as above. Meanwhile, melt 15 g (½ oz) butter in a frying pan, add 125 g (4 oz) baby spinach leaves and cook gently for 2–3 minutes until just wilted. Drain well and dry on kitchen paper. Divide the spinach between the bread cases. Beat together the eggs, cream, cheese and salt and pepper to taste as above and pour over the spinach. Bake in the oven for 15 minutes until set.

freeform spinach, feta & egg tarts

Serves **4**
Preparation time **15 minutes**
Cooking time **20 minutes**

250 g (8 oz) **frozen leaf
  spinach**, thawed
125 g (4 oz) **feta cheese**,
  diced
2 tablespoons **mascarpone
  cheese**
pinch of freshly grated
  nutmeg
4 sheets of **filo pastry**,
  thawed if frozen
50 g (2 oz) **butter**, melted
4 **eggs**
salt and **black pepper**

Drain the spinach and squeeze out all the excess water, then chop finely. Put in a bowl and mix in the feta, mascarpone, nutmeg and salt and pepper to taste.

Lay the sheets of filo pastry on top of one another, brushing each with a little melted butter. Cut out four 15 cm (6 inch) rounds using a saucer as a template.

Divide the spinach mixture between the pastry rounds, spreading the filling out but leaving a 2.5 cm (1 inch) border. Gather the edges up and over the filling to form a rim. Make a shallow well in the spinach mixture.

Transfer the tarts to a baking sheet and bake in a preheated oven, 200°C (400°F), Gas Mark 6, for 8 minutes.

Remove from the oven and carefully crack an egg into each hollow. Return to the oven and bake for a further 8–10 minutes until the eggs are set.

For spinach & goats' cheese parcels, prepare the spinach as above, then mix with 125 g (4 oz) soft goats' cheese, 2 tablespoons mascarpone cheese, a pinch of ground cumin and salt and pepper to taste. Cut out the filo pastry rounds as above and divide the spinach mixture between them, but place it on one half of each round. Carefully fold the pastry over the filling and turn the pastry edges over to seal. Bake in the oven as above and serve with lemon wedges for squeezing over and Greek yogurt.

eggs benedict

Serves **4**
Preparation time **5 minutes**
Cooking time **15 minutes**

8 thick slices of **cooked ham**
4 **muffins** or **brioche**
25 g (1 oz) **butter**
8 hot **poached eggs**
snipped **chives**, to garnish

Hollandaise sauce
3 **egg yolks**
1 tablespoon **cold water**
125 g (4 oz) **butter**,
  softened
large pinch of **salt**
2 pinches of **cayenne
  pepper**
1 teaspoon **lemon juice**
1 tablespoon **single cream**

Warm the ham slices under a preheated high grill for 2–3 minutes on each side. Transfer to an ovenproof dish and keep warm in a low oven.

Make the sauce. Beat the egg yolks and measurement water together in the top of a double boiler over simmering water until the mixture is pale. Gradually add the butter, a small amount at a time, and continue beating until the mixture thickens. Add the salt, 1 pinch of cayenne pepper and lemon juice. Stir in the cream. Remove from the heat and keep warm.

Split the muffins or brioche in half, then toast and spread with the butter. Arrange on warmed plates. Lay a slice of ham on each muffin half and top with a poached egg. Spoon a little of the sauce over each egg. Garnish with the remaining cayenne pepper and chives and serve immediately.

summer berry granola

Serves **4**
Preparation time **10 minutes**
Cooking time **8–9 minutes**

spray olive oil, for oiling
200 g (7 oz) **porridge oats**
100 g (3½ oz) **mixed nuts**,
  toasted and roughly
  chopped
1 tablespoon **maple syrup**,
  plus extra to serve
300 ml (½ pint) **milk**, plus
  extra to serve
150 g (5 oz) **mixed summer
  berries**
Greek yogurt, to serve

Spray a baking sheet lightly with spray oil. Put the oats and nuts in a bowl and stir in the maple syrup. Spread the mixture out on the prepared baking sheet and bake in a preheated oven, 180°C (350°F), Gas Mark 4, for 5 minutes.

Remove from the oven and stir well. Return to the oven and bake for a further 3–4 minutes until lightly toasted. Leave to cool.

Divide the granola between 4 serving bowls and pour over the milk. Add the berries and serve with Greek yogurt and a drizzle of maple syrup.

For Bircher muesli, put the oats and nuts in a bowl and stir in the maple syrup as above, then add 600 ml (1 pint) milk to the oat mixture. Leave to soak for at least 2 hours (or even overnight in the refrigerator) and serve topped with fruits of your choice and natural yogurt.

grilled peaches with passion fruit

Serves **4**
Preparation time **2 minutes**
Cooking time **4–5 minutes**

6 large ripe **peaches**
2 tablespoons **clear honey**,
   plus extra to serve
2 teaspoons **ground
   cinnamon**

To serve
125 g (4 oz) **Greek yogurt**
pulp from 2 **passion fruit**

Cut the peaches in half and discard the stones.
Arrange the peach halves cut side up in a foil-lined grill
pan, drizzle over the honey and dust with the cinnamon.

Cook under a preheated high grill for 4–5 minutes
until lightly charred.

Spoon into serving bowls and serve each one topped
with Greek yogurt, an extra drizzle of honey and the
passion fruit pulp.

For grilled figs with maple syrup & pecans, cut
6 large ripe figs in half and drizzle over 2 tablespoons
maple syrup. Cook under a preheated high grill for
2–3 minutes until softened. Transfer to serving plates
and top each with a spoonful of crème fraîche, a few
toasted chopped pecan nuts and an extra drizzle of
maple syrup.

chilli chocolate chip muffins

Makes **8**
Preparation time **10 minutes**
Cooking time **20 minutes**

200 g (7 oz) **self-raising flour**
50 g (2 oz) **cocoa powder**
1 teaspoon **baking powder**
150 g (5 oz) **soft light brown sugar**
1 **egg**, lightly beaten
250 ml (8 fl oz) **milk**
50 g (2 oz) **butter**, melted
125 g (4 oz) **chilli chocolate**, chopped, or **plain dark chocolate** and a pinch of **chilli powder**
75 g (3 oz) **pecan nuts**, toasted and roughly ground
spray olive oil, for oiling

Cut a 15 cm (6 inch) square from baking paper and use it as a template to cut 7 more. Fold them all into quarters. Open out flat and set aside.

Sift the flour, cocoa powder and baking powder into a bowl and stir in the sugar. Beat together the egg, milk and melted butter in a small bowl, then mix into the dry ingredients until just combined (don't overmix). Fold in the chocolate and pecan nuts.

Spray each square of baking paper with spray oil and press each piece into the hole of a muffin tray. Spoon the chocolate mixture into the lined holes and bake in a preheated oven, 200°C (400°F), Gas Mark 6, for 20 minutes until risen and golden. Leave to cool slightly on a wire rack and serve warm.

For white chocolate & raspberry muffins, sift 250 g (8 oz) self-raising flour and 1 teaspoon baking powder into a bowl and stir in 150 g (5 oz) soft light brown sugar. Beat together 1 lightly beaten egg, 250 ml (8 fl oz) milk and 50 g (2 oz) melted butter, then mix into the dry ingredients until just combined (don't overmix). Fold in 125 g (4 oz) chopped white chocolate and 125 g (4 oz) small raspberries. Bake in the oven as above and serve warm.

soups & one-pot meals

pork chops baked with potatoes

Serves **4**
Preparation time **10 minutes**
Cooking time **45–50 minutes**

750 g (1½ lb) **potatoes**, peeled
2 tablespoons **extra virgin olive oil**
4 large **pork chops**, about 250 g (8 oz) each
125 g (4 oz) **piece of smoked bacon**, rind removed, diced
1 large **onion**, sliced
2 **garlic cloves**, chopped
2 teaspoons **dried oregano**
grated **rind** and **juice** of 1 **lemon**
250 ml (8 fl oz) **chicken stock** (see page 44 for homemade)
salt and **black pepper**
a few **thyme leaves**, to garnish (optional)

Cut the potatoes into 2.5 cm (1 inch) cubes. Heat the oil in an ovenproof frying pan or flameproof casserole, add the pork chops and cook over a high heat for 1–2 minutes on each side until browned. Remove from the pan with a slotted spoon.

Reduce the heat to medium, add the bacon and onion and cook, stirring, for 3–4 minutes until golden. Add the potatoes, garlic, oregano and lemon rind and stir well. Pour in the stock and lemon juice and season lightly with salt and pepper.

Transfer to a preheated oven, 180°C (350°F), Gas Mark 4, and bake, uncovered, for 20 minutes. Arrange the chops on top and bake for a further 20 minutes until the potatoes and pork are cooked through.

For pork chops with roasted sweet potatoes & sage, use 750 g (1½ lb) sweet potatoes, peeled and cut into cubes, instead of the potatoes and cook as above. Continue with the recipe, but use 1 tablespoon chopped sage in place of the dried oregano.

chicken, vegetable & lentil stew

Serves **6**
Preparation time **15 minutes**
Cooking time **2 hours**

1 kg (2 lb) **skinless chicken thigh fillets**, halved
2 tablespoons **plain flour**, seasoned with salt and black pepper
3 tablespoons **olive oil**
1 large **onion**, chopped
2 **carrots**, chopped
2 **celery sticks**, chopped
2 **garlic cloves**, crushed
150 ml (¼ pint) **dry white wine**
1 litre (1¾ pints) **chicken stock** (see below for homemade)
1 tablespoon chopped **rosemary**
150 g (5 oz) **Puy lentils**
salt and **black pepper**

Dust the chicken thighs with the seasoned flour to coat lightly.

Heat half the oil in a flameproof casserole, add the chicken, in 2 batches, and cook over a medium-high heat for 5 minutes until browned on both sides. Remove from the pan with a slotted spoon.

Reduce the heat to medium and add the remaining oil to the pan. Add the onion, carrots, celery, garlic and salt and pepper to taste and cook, stirring frequently, for 5 minutes. Add the wine, stock, rosemary and lentils and return the chicken thighs to the pan.

Bring to the boil, stirring, then reduce the heat, cover and simmer gently for 1½ hours until the vegetables and lentils are tender.

For homemade chicken stock, chop a cooked chicken carcass into 3–4 pieces and put in a large saucepan with any trimmings from the chicken, 1 roughly chopped onion, 2 roughly chopped large carrots, 1 roughly chopped large celery stick, 1 bay leaf, a few lightly crushed parsley stalks, 1 thyme sprig and 1.8 litres (3 pints) cold water. Bring to the boil, skimming off any scum that rises to the surface. Reduce the heat and simmer, uncovered, for 2 hours. Strain through a fine sieve and leave to cool completely before refrigerating. When chilled, remove any solidified fat from the surface. This makes about 1 litre (1¾ pints) stock.

baked cod with tomatoes & olives

Serves **4**
Preparation time **5 minutes**
Cooking time **15 minutes**

250 g (8 oz) **cherry tomatoes**, halved
100 g (3½ oz) **pitted black olives**
2 tablespoons **capers in brine**, drained
4 **thyme sprigs**, plus extra for garnish
4 **cod fillets**, about 175 g (6 oz) each
2 tablespoons **extra virgin olive oil**
2 tablespoons **balsamic vinegar**
salt and **black pepper**

Combine the tomatoes, olives, capers and thyme sprigs in a roasting tin. Nestle the cod fillets in the pan, drizzle over the oil and balsamic vinegar and season to taste with salt and pepper.

Bake in a preheated oven, 200°C (400°F), Gas Mark 6, for 15 minutes.

Transfer the fish, tomatoes and olives to warmed plates. Spoon the pan juices over the fish. Serve immediately with a mixed green leaf salad.

For steamed cod with lemon, arrange a cod fillet on each of 4 x 30 cm (12 inch) squares of foil. Top each with ½ teaspoon grated lemon rind, a squeeze of lemon juice, 1 tablespoon extra virgin olive oil and salt and pepper to taste. Seal the edges of the foil together to form parcels, transfer to a baking sheet and cook in a preheated oven, 200°C (400°F), Gas Mark 6, for 15 minutes. Remove and leave to rest for 5 minutes. Open the parcels and serve sprinkled with chopped parsley.

beef goulash

Serves **8**
Preparation time **10 minutes**
Cooking time **2–2½ hours**

4 tablespoons **olive oil**
1.5 kg (3 lb) **braising steak**, cubed
2 **onions**, sliced
2 **red peppers**, cored, deseeded and diced
1 tablespoon **smoked paprika**
2 tablespoons chopped **marjoram**
1 teaspoon **caraway seeds**
1 litre (1¾ pints) **beef stock** (see below for homemade)
5 tablespoons **tomato purée**
salt and **black pepper**

Heat the oil in a flameproof casserole, add the beef, in 3 batches, and cook over a high heat for 5 minutes until browned all over. Remove from the pan with a slotted spoon.

Add the onions and red peppers to the pan and cook gently for 10 minutes until softened. Stir in the paprika, marjoram and caraway seeds and cook, stirring, for a further 1 minute.

Return the beef to the pan, add the stock, tomato purée and salt and pepper to taste and bring to the boil, stirring. Reduce the heat, cover and simmer gently for 1½–2 hours. You can remove the lid for the final 30 minutes if the sauce needs thickening.

For homemade beef stock, put 750 g (1½ lb) cubed shin of beef, 2 chopped onions, 2–3 chopped carrots, 2 roughly chopped celery sticks, 1 bay leaf, 1 bouquet garni, 4–6 black peppercorns and 1.8 litres (3 pints) cold water in a large saucepan. Slowly bring to the boil, then reduce the heat, cover with a well-fitting lid and simmer gently for 2 hours, skimming off any scum that rises to the surface. Strain through a fine sieve and leave to cool before refrigerating. This makes about 1.5 litres (2½ pints).

treacle & mustard beans

Serves **6**
Preparation time **10 minutes**
Cooking time **1 hour 35 minutes**

1 **carrot**, diced
1 **celery stick**, chopped
1 **onion**, chopped
2 **garlic cloves**, crushed
2 x 400 g (13 oz) cans **soya beans**, drained
700 g (1 lb 7 oz) jar **passata**
75 g (3 oz) **smoked bacon rashers**, diced
2 tablespoons **black treacle**
2 teaspoons **Dijon mustard**
salt and **black pepper**

Put all the ingredients in a flameproof casserole and bring slowly to the boil, stirring occasionally.

Cover, transfer to a preheated oven, 160°C (325°F), Gas Mark 3, and bake for 1 hour.

Remove the lid and bake for a further 30 minutes. Serve with garlic-rubbed bread (see below).

For garlic-rubbed bread to serve with the beans, heat a ridged griddle pan until hot, add 6 thick slices of sourdough bread and cook for 2 minutes on each side until lightly charred. Rub each bread slice with a peeled garlic clove (or 2) and drizzle with extra virgin olive oil.

beef, pickled onion & beer stew

Serves **4**
Preparation time **10 minutes**
Cooking time **2¼ hours**

1 kg (2 lb) **braising steak**, cubed
3 tablespoons **plain flour**, seasoned with salt and black pepper
2 tablespoons **olive oil**
500 g (1 lb) jar **pickled onions**, drained
2 **carrots**, thickly sliced
300 ml (½ pint) **beer**
600 ml (1 pint) **beef stock** (see page 48 for homemade)
4 tablespoons **tomato purée**
1 tablespoon **Worcestershire sauce**
2 **bay leaves**
salt and **black pepper**
few sprigs fresh **parsley**, chopped, to garnish

Dust the beef with the seasoned flour to coat lightly.

Heat the oil in a large flameproof casserole, add the beef, in 3 batches, and cook over a high heat for 5 minutes until browned all over, removing from the pan with a slotted spoon. Return all the beef to the pan.

Add the onions and carrots to the pan and stir well, then gradually stir in the beer and stock and bring to the boil. Stir in the tomato purée, Worcestershire sauce, bay leaves and salt and pepper to taste.

Cover, transfer to a preheated oven, 160°C (325°F), Gas Mark 3, and cook for 2 hours, stirring halfway through, until the beef and vegetables are tender. Garnish with the parsley and serve with soft polenta (see below).

For soft polenta to serve with the stew, bring 1 litre (1¾ pints) water to a rolling boil in a saucepan, add 2 teaspoons salt and gradually whisk in 175 g (6 oz) polenta, stirring constantly until the mixture boils. Cook for 5 minutes, remove from the heat and stir in 50 g (2 oz) butter and 4 tablespoons freshly grated Parmesan cheese. Add salt and pepper to taste.

chicken & rice bake

Serves **4**
Preparation time **15 minutes**
Cooking time **1 hour**

8 skinless **chicken thighs
   fillets**, about 750 g (1½ lb)
   in total
8 **streaky bacon rashers**,
   rind removed
2 tablespoons **olive oil**
250 g (8 oz) **long-grain rice**
1 **onion**, chopped
2 **garlic cloves**, crushed
1 teaspoon **ground turmeric**
grated **rind** and **juice** of
   ½ **lemon**
500 ml (17 fl oz) hot **chicken
   stock** (see page 44 for
   homemade)
1 tablespoon chopped **fresh
   coriander**
salt and **black pepper**

Wrap each chicken thigh with a bacon rasher and
secure in place with a cocktail stick.

Heat the oil in a flameproof casserole, add the chicken
and cook over a high heat for 5 minutes until browned
all over. Remove with a slotted spoon.

Add the rice to the pan and cook over a low heat,
stirring, for 1 minute. Add the onion, garlic, turmeric,
lemon rind, stock and salt and pepper to taste. Arrange
the chicken thighs over the rice, pressing down gently.

Cover with a layer of foil, then the lid. Transfer to a
preheated oven, 180°C (350°F), Gas Mark 4, and bake
for 50 minutes.

Remove from the oven and stir in the coriander and
lemon juice. Discard the cocktail sticks and serve with
a tangy yogurt sauce (see below).

For tangy yogurt sauce to serve with the rice,
combine 150 g (5 oz) Greek yogurt with 1 teaspoon
grated lemon rind, 1 crushed garlic clove, 2 teaspoons
lemon juice, 1 tablespoon chopped parsley and salt
and pepper to taste in a bowl.

pumpkin soup with crispy bacon

Serves **4**
Preparation time **10 minutes**
Cooking time **30 minutes**

1 kg (2 lb) **pumpkin**, peeled and deseeded
2 tablespoons **extra virgin olive oil**
1 large **onion**, sliced
2 **garlic cloves**, crushed
½ teaspoon **smoked paprika**
1¼ litre (2 pints) **chicken stock** (see page 44 for homemade)
4 **streaky bacon rashers**, rind removed
salt and **black pepper**

Cut the pumpkin into 2.5 cm (1 inch) cubes and put in a roasting tin. Add 1 tablespoon olive oil and stir well. Roast in a preheated oven, 200°C (400°F), Gas Mark 6, for 25 minutes.

Meanwhile, heat 1 tablespoon olive oil in a large saucepan, add the onion, garlic, paprika and a little salt and pepper and cook gently for 10 minutes until soft.

Add the cooked pumpkin and stock to the pan, bring to the boil and cook for 5 minutes. Transfer to a food processor or blender and process until smooth.

Meanwhile, cook the bacon under a preheated high grill until crisp.

Spoon the soup into warmed bowls. Break the bacon into small pieces and scatter on top, and drizzle the remaining oil over the soup.

For pumpkin soup with olive salsa, combine 125 g (4 oz) chopped pitted black olives, 2 tablespoons extra virgin olive oil, grated rind of ½ lemon, 1 tablespoon chopped parsley and pepper to taste in a bowl. Make the pumpkin soup as above and serve topped with the olive salsa.

garlic, paprika & egg soup

Serves **4**
Preparation time **10 minutes**
Cooking time **20 minutes**

4 tablespoons **olive oil**
12 thick slices of **baguette**
5 **garlic cloves**, sliced
1 **onion**, finely chopped
1 tablespoon **paprika**
1 teaspoon **ground cumin**
good pinch of **saffron
  threads**
1.2 litres (2 pints) **vegetable
  stock** (see below for
  homemade)
25 g (1 oz) **dried soup pasta**
4 **eggs**
salt and **black pepper**

Heat the oil in a heavy-based saucepan, add the bread slices and cook gently, turning once, until golden. Remove from the pan with a slotted spoon and drain on kitchen paper.

Add the garlic, onion, paprika and cumin to the pan and cook gently, stirring, for 3 minutes. Add the saffron and stock and bring to the boil. Stir in the soup pasta. Reduce the heat, cover and simmer for about 8 minutes, or until the pasta is just tender. Season to taste with salt and pepper.

Break the eggs on to a saucer and slide into the pan, one at a time. Cook for about 2 minutes, or until poached.

Stack 3 fried bread slices in each of 4 warmed soup bowls. Ladle the soup over the bread, making sure that each serving contains an egg. Serve immediately.

For homemade vegetable stock, put 625 g (1¼ lb) chopped mixed vegetables, such as carrots, leeks, celery, onions and mushrooms, 1 garlic clove, peeled but left whole, 8 black peppercorns, 1 bouquet garni and 1.5 litres (2½ pints) cold water in a large saucepan. Bring to the boil, then reduce the heat and simmer gently, uncovered, for 30 minutes, skimming off any scum that rises to the surface. Strain the stock through a fine sieve and leave to cool completely before refrigerating. This will make around 1.2 litres (2 pints) stock.

chicken noodle soup

Serves **4**
Preparation time **10 minutes**,
  plus cooling
Cooking time **40 minutes**

2 **chicken quarters**, about
  750 g (1½ lb) in total
1 **onion**, chopped
4 **garlic cloves**, chopped
3 slices of **fresh root ginger**,
  peeled and bruised
2 litres (3½ pints) **cold water**
125 g (4 oz) **dried egg
  thread noodles**
2 tablespoons **light soy
  sauce**
1 **red bird's eye chilli**,
  deseeded and sliced
2 **spring onions**, sliced
2 tablespoons **fresh
  coriander leaves**
salt and **black pepper**

Put the chicken quarters, onion, garlic, ginger, measurement water and salt and pepper to taste in a saucepan. Bring to the boil, then reduce the heat and simmer gently, uncovered, for 30 minutes, skimming off any scum that rises to the surface.

Remove the chicken and strain the stock. Leave to cool, and meanwhile skin the chicken and shred the flesh.

Cook the noodles in boiling water for 6 minutes. Drain well and divide between 4 bowls.

Heat the stock in a saucepan with the soy sauce. Add the chicken and simmer for 5 minutes.

Spoon the stock and chicken over the noodles and sprinkle over the chilli, spring onion slices and coriander leaves. Serve immediately.

For Thai chicken noodle soup, cook the chicken quarters with the other ingredients in the water as above, adding 6 large torn kaffir lime leaves. Remove the chicken and strain the stock. When cool, skin the chicken and shred as above. Heat the stock in a saucepan with 2 tablespoons Thai fish sauce, juice of ½ lime, 2 teaspoons caster sugar and 1 deseeded and sliced red bird's eye chilli. Add the chicken and simmer for 5 minutes. Meanwhile, put 125 g (4 oz) dried rice noodles in a large heatproof bowl, pour over enough boiling water to cover and leave to stand for 5 minutes until just tender, then drain. Serve the noodles with the stock and chicken spooned over, garnished with sliced chillies, coriander leaves and shredded kaffir lime leaves.

gazpacho

Serves **4**
Preparation time **10 minutes**,
  plus chilling
Cooking time **25 minutes**

750 g (1½ lb) ripe **tomatoes**
1 large **fennel bulb**
300 ml (½ pint) **salted boiling water**
¾ teaspoon **coriander seeds**
½ teaspoon **mixed peppercorns**
1 tablespoon **extra virgin olive oil**
1 large **garlic clove**, crushed
1 small **onion**, chopped
1 tablespoon **balsamic vinegar**
1 tablespoon **lemon juice**
¾ teaspoon chopped **oregano**, plus extra leaves to garnish
1 teaspoon **tomato purée**
1 rounded teaspoon **rock salt**
green olives, finely sliced, to garnish

Put the tomatoes in a large saucepan or heatproof bowl and pour over enough boiling water to cover, then leave for about 1 minute. Drain, skin the tomatoes carefully and roughly chop the flesh.

Trim the green fronds from the fennel and discard. Finely slice the bulb, put in a saucepan and pour over the measurement salted boiling water. Cover and simmer for 10 minutes.

Meanwhile, crush the coriander seeds and peppercorns in a mortar with a pestle. Heat the oil in a large saucepan, add the crushed spices, garlic and onion and cook gently for 5 minutes.

Add the vinegar, lemon juice, tomatoes and chopped oregano to the onion mixture. Stir well and then add the fennel and its cooking water, the tomato purée and salt. Bring to a simmer and leave to cook, uncovered, for 10 minutes.

Transfer to a food processor or blender and process to preferred consistency. Leave to cool, then chill overnight or for at least several hours. Serve garnished with the oregano leaves and olive slices.

For roasted tomato gazpacho place 750 g (1½ lb) halved tomatoes in a roasting tin with 2 tablespoons extra virgin olive oil and little salt and pepper to taste. Roast in a preheated oven 200°C (400°F), Gas Mark 6, for 25 minutes until roasted. Leave to cool and then, following the above recipe, process with the remaining ingredients replacing the oregano with 1 tablespoon chopped fresh basil. Chill for 1 hour before serving.

pea, lettuce & lemon soup

Serves **4**
Preparation time **10 minutes**
Cooking time **20 minutes**

25 g (1 oz) **butter**
1 large **onion**, finely
  chopped
425 g (14 oz) **frozen peas**
2 **Little Gem lettuces**,
  roughly chopped
1 litre (1¾ pints) **vegetable**
  or **chicken stock** (see
  pages 58 and 44 for
  homemade)
grated **rind** and **juice** of
  ½ **lemon**
salt and **black pepper**

Sesame croûtons
2 thick slices of **multigrain
  bread**, cubed
1 tablespoon **olive oil**
1 tablespoon **sesame seeds**

Make the croûtons. Brush the bread cubes with the
oil and spread out in a roasting tin. Sprinkle with
the sesame seeds and bake in a preheated oven,
200°C (400°F), Gas Mark 6, for 10–15 minutes,
or until golden.

Meanwhile, melt the butter in a large saucepan,
add the onion and cook gently for 5 minutes, or
until softened. Add the peas, lettuce, stock, lemon
rind and juice and salt and pepper to taste. Bring to
the boil, then reduce the heat, cover and simmer for
10–15 minutes.

Leave the soup to cool slightly, then transfer to a food
processor or blender and process until smooth. Return
the soup to the pan, adjust the seasoning if necessary
and reheat gently. Spoon into warmed serving bowls
and sprinkle with the croûtons.

For ricotta & mint croûtons instead of the sesame
croûtons, cut 8 thin slices of baguette and lightly toast
under a preheated medium grill for 2 minutes on each
side until golden. Rub over each side with a peeled
garlic clove and drizzle with 1 tablespoon extra virgin
olive oil. Spread the toasts with 125 g (4 oz) ricotta
cheese and arrange 2 on each soup serving. Scatter
over 2 tablespoons sliced mint leaves, season to taste
with salt and pepper and drizzle with a little extra oil.

chilli bean & red pepper soup

Serves **6**
Preparation time **20 minutes**
Cooking time **40 minutes**

2 tablespoons **sunflower oil**
1 large **onion**, finely chopped
4 **garlic cloves**, finely
  chopped
2 **red peppers**, cored,
  deseeded and diced
2 **red chillies**, deseeded and
  finely chopped
900 ml (1½ pints) **vegetable
  stock** (see page 58 for
  homemade)
750 ml (1¼ pints) **tomato
  juice** or **passata**
2 tablespoons **sweet chilli
  sauce**, or more to taste
400 g (13 oz) can **red kidney
  beans**, drained
2 tablespoons finely chopped
  fresh coriander
salt and **black pepper**
rind of 1 **lime**, cut into strips,
  to garnish (optional)

To serve
75 ml (3 fl oz) **soured cream**
  or **crème fraîche**
tortilla chips

Heat the oil in a large saucepan, add the onion and garlic and cook gently for 5 minutes, or until softened but not coloured. Stir in the red peppers and chillies and cook for a few minutes. Stir in the stock and tomato juice or passata, chilli sauce, beans, coriander and salt and pepper to taste. Bring to the boil, then reduce the heat, cover and simmer for 30 minutes.

Leave to cool slightly, then transfer to a food processor or blender and process until smooth. Return the soup to the pan and adjust the seasoning, adding a little extra chilli sauce if necessary. Reheat gently.

Spoon into warmed soup bowls. Stir a little soured cream or crème fraîche into each portion and garnish with lime rind strips, if wished. Serve with tortilla chips.

For crispy sliced tortilla wedges to serve with the soup, cut each of 2 large flour tortillas into 12 wedges. Spray with olive oil spray and season with salt, pepper and a little cayenne pepper. Lay on a grill rack, spice-side up, and toasted under a preheated medium grill for 1–2 minutes until crisp.

20-minute suppers

pork cutlets with caramel pears

Serves **4**
Preparation time **5 minutes**
Cooking time **15–20 minutes**

2 **William pears**, cored and
    thickly sliced
2 tablespoons **soft light
    brown sugar**
4 **pork cutlets**, about 250 g
    (8 oz) each
50 g (2 oz) **unsalted butter**
12 large **sage leaves**
250 ml (8 fl oz) **hot chicken
    stock** (see page 44 for
    homemade)
salt and **black pepper**

Toss the pear slices with the sugar and set aside.
Season the pork cutlets with salt and pepper.

Melt half the butter in a frying pan, add the sage
leaves and cook over a high heat for about 3 minutes,
or until crisp. Remove from the pan with a slotted
spoon and set aside.

Add the cutlets to the pan and cook over a medium
heat for 3–4 minutes on each side, or until golden.
Remove from the pan, cover loosely with foil and
keep warm.

Melt the remaining butter in the pan, add the pear
slices and cook for 2 minutes until golden. Remove
from the pan with a slotted spoon and set aside with
the chops.

Pour the stock into the pan and simmer gently for
2–3 minutes, or until reduced and thickened slightly.
Serve the chops and pear slices with the sauce,
garnished with the crispy sage.

For French beans with garlic & lemon to serve as an
accompaniment, blanch 375 g (12 oz) French beans
in a saucepan of salted boiling water for 2 minutes.
Drain and refresh under cold water. Drain again and
pat dry. Heat 2 tablespoons extra virgin olive oil in a
large frying pan, add 2 sliced garlic cloves and cook
gently, stirring, for 3 minutes until soft. Stir in the
beans and a squeeze of lemon juice and season to
taste with salt and pepper.

asian chicken parcels

Serves **4**
Preparation time **5 minutes**
Cooking time **15 minutes**

4 **skinless chicken breast
fillets**, about 250 g (8 oz)
each
75 ml (3 fl oz) **light soy
sauce**
1 tablespoon **clear honey**
2 **garlic cloves**, sliced
2 **red chillies**, deseeded and
finely chopped
2.5 cm (1 inch) piece of
fresh root ginger, peeled
and finely shredded
4 **star anise**
3 **baby pak choi**, quartered

Score each chicken breast several times with a knife
and put one on each of 4 x 30 cm (12 inch) squares
of foil.

Combine the soy sauce, honey, garlic, chillies,
ginger and star anise in a small bowl, then spoon
over the chicken.

Arrange 3 pak choi quarters on top of the chicken
breasts. Seal the edges of the foil together to form
parcels, transfer to a baking sheet and bake in a
preheated oven, 200°C (400°F), Gas Mark 6, for
15 minutes until the chicken is cooked through.

Leave to rest for 5 minutes, then serve the parcels
with boiled jasmine rice.

For Mediterranean chicken parcels, score the
chicken breasts as above, put on the foil squares and
season with salt and pepper. Top with 2 teaspoons
dried oregano, 2 chopped tomatoes, 50 g (2 oz)
chopped pitted black olives, 2 tablespoons drained
capers in brine and a good drizzle of extra virgin olive
oil. Cook in the oven as above and serve with a mixed
leaf salad and some crusty bread.

vegetable & tofu stir-fry

Serves **4**
Preparation time **10 minutes**
Cooking time **7 minutes**

3 tablespoons **sunflower oil**
300 g (10 oz) **firm tofu**,
  cubed
1 **onion**, sliced
2 **carrots**, sliced
150 g (5 oz) **broccoli**,
  broken into small florets
  and stalks sliced
1 **red pepper**, cored,
  deseeded and sliced
1 large **courgette**, sliced
150 g (5 oz) **sugar snap
  peas**
2 tablespoons **soy sauce**
2 tablespoons **sweet chilli
  sauce**
125 ml (4 fl oz) **water**

To garnish
chopped **red chillies**
Thai or **ordinary basil leaves**

Heat 1 tablespoon of the oil in a wok or large frying pan until starting to smoke, add the tofu and stir-fry over a high heat for 2 minutes until golden. Remove from the pan with a slotted spoon.

Heat the remaining oil in the pan, add the onion and carrots and stir-fry for 1½ minutes. Add the broccoli and red pepper and stir-fry for 1 minute, then add the courgette and sugar snap peas and stir-fry for 1 minute.

Combine the soy and chilli sauces and measurement water and add to the pan with the tofu. Cook for 1 minute. Serve in bowls, garnished with chopped red chillies and basil leaves.

For sesame noodles to serve as an accompaniment, put 375 g (12 oz) egg thread noodles in a large heatproof bowl, pour over enough boiling water to cover and leave to stand for 4 minutes until just tender. Drain well, then toss with 1 tablespoon light soy sauce and 2 teaspoons sesame oil. Serve sprinkled with 1 tablespoon toasted sesame seeds.

asian tuna salad

Serves **4**
Preparation time **10 minutes**,
   plus marinating
Cooking time **1 minute**

375 g (12 oz) **fresh tuna
   steak**, cut into strips
3 tablespoons **soy sauce**
1 teaspoon **wasabi paste**
1 tablespoon **sake** or **dry
   white wine**
200 g (7 oz) **mixed salad
   leaves**
150 g (5 oz) **baby yellow
   tomatoes**, halved
1 **cucumber**, sliced into wide
   fine strips

Dressing
2 tablespoons **soy sauce**
1 tablespoon **lime juice**
1 teaspoon **brown sugar**
2 teaspoons **sesame oil**

Combine the tuna with the soy sauce, wasabi and sake or wine in a bowl. Cover and leave to marinate for 10 minutes.

Arrange the salad leaves, tomatoes and cucumber on serving plates.

Make the dressing. Put all the ingredients in a bowl and whisk together with a fork or put in a screw-top jar and shake to combine.

Heat a dry nonstick pan over a high heat, add the tuna and cook for about 10 seconds on each side or until seared. Place the tuna on top of the salad, drizzle with the dressing and serve.

For Thai tuna salad, leave the tuna steak whole and omit the marinating. Heat a ridged griddle pan until very hot, add the tuna and cook over a high heat for 30 seconds on each side. Remove from the pan and leave to rest briefly. Meanwhile, whisk together 1 tablespoon Thai fish sauce, 1 tablespoon lime juice and 2 teaspoons caster sugar in a bowl, then add 1 finely sliced red chilli and 1 crushed garlic clove. Slice the tuna thinly and arrange over the salad leaves, tomatoes and cucumber on serving plates as above. Drizzle over the dressing and serve.

thai chicken curry

Serves **4**
Preparation time **5 minutes**
Cooking time **15 minutes**

1 tablespoon **sunflower oil**
1 tablespoon **Thai green curry paste** (see below for homemade)
6 **kaffir lime leaves**, torn
2 tablespoons **Thai fish sauce**
1 tablespoon **soft light brown sugar**
200 ml (7 fl oz) **chicken stock**
400 ml (13 fl oz) can **coconut milk**
500 g (1 lb) **skinless chicken thigh fillets**, diced
125 g (4 oz) can **bamboo shoots**, drained
125 g (4 oz) can **baby sweetcorn**
1 large handful **Thai basil leaves** or **fresh coriander leaves**, plus extra to garnish
1 tablespoon **lime juice**
1 **red chilli**, sliced, to garnish

Heat the oil in a wok or large frying pan, add the curry paste and lime leaves and stir-fry over a low heat for 1–2 minutes until fragrant.

Add the fish sauce, sugar, stock and coconut milk and bring to the boil, then reduce the heat and simmer gently for 5 minutes.

Add the chicken and cook for 5 minutes. Add the bamboo shoots and baby sweetcorn and cook for a further 3 minutes.

Stir through the basil or coriander leaves and lime juice, then serve garnished with the leaves and chilli.

For homemade Thai green curry paste, put 15 small green chillies, 4 halved garlic cloves, 2 finely chopped lemon grass stalks, 2 torn Kaffir lime leaves, 2 chopped shallots, 2.5 cm (1 inch) piece of peeled and finely chopped fresh root ginger, 2 teaspoons black peppercorns, 1 teaspoon pared lime rind, ½ teaspoon salt and 1 tablespoon groundnut oil in a food processor or blender and process to a thick paste. Transfer to a screw-top jar. This makes about 150 ml (¼ pint) of paste, which can be stored in the refrigerator for up to 3 weeks.

seared beef & broccoli bruschetta

Serves **4**
Preparation time **5 minutes**
Cooking time **10 minutes**

375 g (12 oz) **broccoli florets**
500 g (1 lb) **sirloin steak**
75 ml (3 fl oz) **extra virgin olive oil**
4 slices of **sourdough bread**
2 **garlic cloves**, sliced
1 small **red chilli**, deseeded and finely chopped
1 tablespoon **balsamic vinegar**
125 g (4 oz) **baby rocket leaves**
salt and **black pepper**

Blanch the broccoli in a saucepan of lightly salted boiling water for 2 minutes. Drain well and refresh under cold water. Drain again, pat dry and set aside.

Rub the beef with 1 tablespoon of the oil and season well with salt and pepper.

Heat a ridged griddle pan until very hot, add the beef and cook over a high heat for 2 minutes on each side. Remove and leave to rest for 5 minutes, then cut into thick slices.

While the beef is resting, reheat the griddle pan, add the sourdough bread slices and cook for 2 minutes on each side until lightly charred.

Heat the remaining oil in a wok or large frying pan, add the garlic and chilli and stir-fry for 1 minute. Add the broccoli and stir-fry for 1 minute. Stir in the vinegar and remove from heat. Combine with the beef and rocket in a large bowl.

Arrange the bread on serving plates, top with the beef salad and serve.

For beef bruschetta with horseradish dressing, prepare and cook the beef as above. While the beef is resting, lightly chargrill the sourdough bread as above. Combine the sliced beef with 125 g (4 oz) picked watercress leaves in a large bowl. Arrange the bread on serving plates and top with the beef and watercress. Beat together 2 tablespoons soured cream, 2 teaspoons horseradish sauce, 1 teaspoon white wine vinegar and salt and pepper to taste. Drizzle over the bruschetta and serve.

soy & orange salmon with noodles

Serves **4**
Preparation time **5 minutes**
Cooking time **15 minutes**

4 **skinless salmon fillets**,
    about 175 g (6 oz) each
spray olive oil, for oiling
250 g (8 oz) **dried soba
    noodles**
4 tablespoons **dark soy
    sauce**
2 tablespoons **orange juice**
2 tablespoons **mirin** (rice
    wine seasoning)
2 teaspoons **sesame oil**
2 tablespoons **sesame
    seeds**

Remove any bones from the salmon fillets and put the salmon in a bowl.

Heat a heavy-based frying pan until hot and spray lightly with spray oil. Add the salmon and cook for 3–4 minutes on each side until browned. Remove, wrap loosely in foil and leave to rest for 5 minutes.

Meanwhile, plunge the noodles into a large saucepan of boiling water. Return to the boil and cook for about 5 minutes, or until just tender. Drain well and toss with the sesame oil and seeds.

While the noodles are cooking, combine the soy sauce, orange juice and mirin. Pour into the frying pan and bring to the boil, then reduce the heat and simmer for 1 minute.

Divide the noodles between serving bowls and top each with the salmon and sauce. Serve with steamed sugar snap peas.

For salmon, orange & soy parcels, put each salmon fillet on a 30 cm (12 inch) square of foil. Draw the foil edges up to form 'cups' and add the soy sauce, orange juice and mirin as above, along with 2 sliced spring onions, 2 sliced garlic cloves and 2 teaspoons grated fresh root ginger. Seal the edges of the foil together to form parcels, transfer to a baking sheet and bake in a preheated oven, 200°C (400°F), Gas Mark 6, for 15 minutes. Remove and leave to rest briefly, then serve with steamed rice.

lamb with olive & pine nut salsa

Serves **4**
Preparation time **10 minutes**
Cooking time **9 minutes**

4 **lamb loin chops**, about
   200 g (7 oz) each
1 tablespoon **extra virgin
   olive oil**
4 teaspoons **dried oregano**

Olive & pine nut salsa
3 tablespoons **extra virgin
   olive oil**
25 g (1 oz) **pine nuts**,
   toasted
125 g (4 oz) **pitted black
   olives**, halved
2 tablespoons drained
   capers in brine
2 tablespoons chopped
   parsley
1 tablespoon **lemon juice**
salt and **black pepper**
rocket leaves, to garnish

Make the salsa. Heat 1 tablespoon of the oil in a small frying pan, add the pine nuts and cook gently for 30 seconds until golden. Leave to cool.

Combine the cooled pine nuts with the olives, capers, parsley, lemon juice and remaining oil in a bowl and season to taste with salt and pepper.

Brush the chops with the oil and season with the oregano and salt and pepper. Heat a ridged griddle pan until hot, add the chops and cook for 4 minutes on each side.

Remove the chops from the pan, wrap loosely in foil and leave to rest for 5 minutes. Serve with the salsa.

For lamb chops with tomato, mint & feta salad, follow the recipe above to cook the chops. Meanwhile, combine 4 diced tomatoes, 1 crushed garlic clove, 125 g (4 oz) crumbled feta cheese, 50 g (2 oz) pitted black olives, 2 tablespoons chopped mint leaves, 2 tablespoons extra virgin olive oil, 2 teaspoons balsamic vinegar and salt and pepper to taste in a bowl. Stir well and serve with the lamb.

chicken & hummus wraps

Serves **4**
Preparation time **5 minutes**
Cooking time **10 minutes**

6 **skinless chicken thigh**
   fillets, about 500 g (1 lb)
   in total
2 tablespoons **extra virgin**
   olive oil
grated **rind** and **juice** of
   1 lemon
1 **garlic clove**, crushed
1 teaspoon **ground cumin**
4 **flour tortillas**
200 g (7 oz) shop-bought
   hummus (see below for
   homemade)
25 g (1 oz) **wild rocket**
   leaves
1 handful **parsley leaves**
salt and **black pepper**

Cut the chicken thighs into quarters and put in a bowl.
Combine the oil, lemon rind, garlic, cumin and salt and
pepper to taste, add to the chicken and stir well.

Heat a ridged griddle pan until hot. Thread the chicken
pieces on to metal skewers, add to the pan and cook
for 4–5 minutes on each side. Remove and leave to
rest for 5 minutes.

Meanwhile, warm the tortillas in a preheated oven,
150°C (350°F), Gas Mark 2, for 5 minutes.

Remove the chicken from the skewers. Divide the
hummus, rocket leaves, parsley and chicken between
the tortillas. Squeeze over the lemon juice, wrap
and serve.

For easy homemade hummus, put 400 g (13 oz)
can chickpeas, drained, 1 crushed garlic clove,
3 tablespoons extra virgin olive oil, 1 tablespoon
lemon juice and salt and pepper to taste in a food
processor or blender and process until smooth.

hoisin pork stir-fry

Serves **2**
Preparation time **8 minutes**
Cooking time **6–8 minutes**

1 tablespoon **hoisin sauce**
1 tablespoon **light soy sauce**
1 tablespoon **white wine vinegar**
1 tablespoon **vegetable oil**
2 **garlic cloves**, sliced
1 teaspoon grated **fresh root ginger**
1 small **red chilli**, deseeded and sliced
250 g (8 oz) **pork fillet**, thinly sliced
175 g (6 oz) **sugar snap peas**
175 g (6 oz) **broccoli florets**
2 tablespoons **water**

Combine the hoisin and soy sauces and vinegar in a bowl and set aside.

Heat the oil in a wok or large frying pan until starting to smoke, add the garlic, ginger and chilli and stir-fry over a high heat for 10 seconds. Add the pork fillet and stir-fry for 2–3 minutes until golden. Remove with a slotted spoon.

Add the sugar snap peas and broccoli florets to the pan and stir-fry for 1 minute. Add the measurement water and cook for a further 1 minute.

Return the pork to the pan, add the sauce mixture and cook for 1 minute until the vegetables are cooked. Serve with steamed rice.

For roasted hoisin pork, make the hoisin mixture as above. Brush the sauce over 4 pieces of pork fillet, about 175 g (6 oz) each, in a roasting tin and roast in a preheated oven, 200°C (400°F), Gas Mark 6, for 15 minutes. Leave to rest for 5 minutes, then serve with steamed green vegetables and boiled rice.

tuna & pesto burgers

Serves **4**
Preparation time **5 minutes**
Cooking time **4–6 minutes**

4 **ciabatta rolls**
4 **fresh tuna steaks**, about 175 g (6 oz) each
1 tablespoon **extra virgin olive oil**, plus extra to drizzle
1 **lemon**, halved
2 **tomatoes**, sliced
4 tablespoons **basil pesto**
50 g (2 oz) **mixed salad leaves**
salt and **black pepper**

Heat a ridged griddle pan until hot. Split the rolls in half, add to pan and cook for 1–2 minutes on each side until lightly charred. Transfer to serving plates.

Brush the tuna steaks lightly with the oil and season with salt and pepper. Add to the pan and cook for 1 minute on each side.

Transfer each tuna steak to the base of a roll and squeeze over a little lemon juice from the lemon halves. Divide the tomato slices, pesto and salad leaves between the roll bases and drizzle over a little extra oil. Replace the roll tops and serve immediately.

For chicken & sweet chilli burgers, split and lightly char the rolls on a hot ridged griddle pan as above. Cut 2 large skinless chicken breast fillets in half horizontally to give 4 thinner fillets. Brush the chicken with 1 tablespoon extra virgin olive oil and season with salt and pepper. Add to the hot pan and cook for 3 minutes on each side. Transfer a piece of chicken to each roll half and add 1 tablespoon sweet chilli sauce and a small handful of mixed salad leaves.

mussels with cider

Serves **2**
Preparation time **10 minutes**
Cooking time **9 minutes**

1.5 kg (3 lb) small **farmed
    mussels**
2 **garlic cloves**, chopped
150 ml (¼ pint) **dry cider**
100 g (3½ oz) **double cream**
2 tablespoons chopped
    parsley
salt and **black pepper**

Wash the mussels thoroughly and put in a large saucepan with the garlic and cider. Bring to the boil, cover and cook over a medium heat for 4–5 minutes until all the shells have opened. Discard any that remain closed after cooking.

Strain the mussels through a colander and put in a large bowl, cover with foil and place in a very low oven to keep warm.

Pass the cooking juices through a fine sieve into a clean saucepan and bring to the boil. Whisk in the cream and simmer for 3–4 minutes, or until thickened slightly. Season to taste with salt and pepper.

Pour the sauce over the mussels, scatter over the parsley and serve immediately with plenty of crusty French bread to mop up the juices.

For mussels with Asian flavours, wash the mussels thoroughly and put in a large saucepan with 2 sliced garlic cloves, 2 teaspoons grated fresh root ginger, 4 sliced spring onions and 1 sliced red chilli. Add a splash of water and cook as above. Strain the mussels and keep warm. Strain the cooking juices through a fine sieve into a clean saucepan. Whisk in 100 g (3½ oz) coconut cream and heat through. Pour over the mussels and served garnished with chopped fresh coriander.

mustard & tarragon pork steaks

Serves **4**
Preparation time **5 minutes**
Cooking time **10–12 minutes**

8 **pork steaks**, about 100 g
   (3½ oz) each
15 g **butter**
1 tablespoon **extra virgin
   olive oil**
150 ml (¼ pint) **chicken
   stock**
120 ml (4 fl oz) **double
   cream**
4 teaspoons **wholegrain
   mustard**
1 tablespoon **chopped fresh
   tarragon**
salt and **black pepper**

Season the steaks on both sides with salt and pepper.

Heat the butter and oil together in a large frying pan and as soon as the butter stops foaming add the chops. Cook over a medium heat for 3–4 minutes each side until golden. Remove from the pan and wrap loosely in foil. Rest for 5 minutes.

Add the stock to the pan and simmer for 3 minutes then stir in the cream and mustard and simmer gently for 1–2 minutes until thickened slightly. Add the tarragon and remove from the heat.

Arrange the pork on plates, pour over the sauce and serve with some steamed green vegetables, if liked.

For mustard & honey chicken, combine 1 tablespoon wholegrain mustard, 1 tablespoon clear honey and some salt and pepper. Brush over 4 skinless chicken breast fillets and bake in a preheated over 200°C (400°F) Gas Mark 6 for 15 minutes. Serve with green beans.

chilli thai beef baguettes

Serves **4**
Preparation time **5 minutes**
Cooking time **4 minutes**

500 g (1 lb) **thick sirloin
steak**, trimmed
1 tablespoon **olive oil**
4 **oval bread rolls**
4 **fresh coriander sprigs**
4 **Thai** or **ordinary basil
sprigs**
4 **mint sprigs**

Dressing
2 tablespoons **Thai fish
sauce**
2 tablespoons **lime juice**
2 tablespoons **light soft
brown sugar**
1 large **red chilli**, thinly sliced
salt and **black pepper**

Heat a ridged griddle pan until very hot. Brush the steak with the oil and season liberally with salt and pepper. Add the steak to the pan and cook over a high heat for 2 minutes on each side, making sure that you sear all over. Leave to rest for 5 minutes, then cut into thin slices. The steak should be rare.

Meanwhile, make the dressing. Place the fish sauce, lime juice and sugar in a bowl and stir in the chilli until the sugar has dissolved.

Split the rolls in half and fill with the herbs, beef slices and any juices. Pour the dressing carefully over and serve.

For Thai beef salad, cook, rest and slice the steak as above. Toss with 1 sliced Lebanese cucumber, 250 g (8 oz) halved cherry tomatoes, 100 g (3½ oz) bean sprouts and 1 handful each of Thai or ordinary basil, fresh coriander and mint leaves in a bowl. Combine the juice of ½ lime, 1 teaspoon sesame oil, 1 teaspoon caster sugar, 1 teaspoon Thai fish sauce and 1 tablespoon groundnut oil. Add to the salad, toss well until evenly coated and serve.

tortilla pizza with salami

Makes **2**
Preparation time **5 minutes**
Cooking time **8–10 minutes**
  per pizza

2 large **flour tortillas** or
  flatbreads
4 tablespoons shop-bought
  tomato pasta sauce
100 g (3½ oz) **spicy salami
  slices**
150 g (5 oz) **mozzarella
  cheese**, thinly sliced
1 tablespoon **oregano
  leaves**, plus extra to
  garnish
salt and **black pepper**

Lay the tortillas or flatbreads on 2 large baking sheets. Top each with half the pasta sauce, spreading it up to the edge. Arrange half the salami and mozzarella slices and oregano leaves over the top.

Bake in a preheated oven, 200°C (400°F), Gas Mark 6, for 8–10 minutes until the cheese is melted and golden. Serve garnished with extra oregano leaves.

For spicy salami, mozzarella & tomato quesadilla, lay 1 large flour tortilla or flatbread on the work surface. Top with 2 tablespoons tomato pasta sauce, 50 g (2 oz) salami slices, 75 g (3 oz) diced mozzarella cheese and a few basil leaves. Add a second tortilla and press flat. Heat a large frying pan or ridged griddle pan until hot, add the quesadilla and cook for 2–3 minutes until toasted. Flip over and cook on the second side. Cut into wedges to serve.

chilli & lemon prawns with pasta

Serves **2**
Preparation time **5 minutes**,
  plus marinating
Cooking time **3 minutes**

3 tablespoons **extra virgin
  olive oil**, plus extra for
  stir-frying
2 large **garlic cloves**,
  crushed
1 large **red chilli**, deseeded
  and chopped
grated **rind** and **juice** of
  1 lemon
375 g (12 oz) large **raw
  peeled prawns**
250 g (8 oz) **fresh spaghetti**
4 **spring onions**, sliced
2 tablespoons chopped
  basil
salt and **black pepper**

Combine the oil, garlic, chilli, lemon rind and salt and
pepper to taste in a non-metallic bowl, add the prawns
and stir well. Cover and leave to marinate in the
refrigerator for 1 hour.

Cook the pasta in a large saucepan of salted boiling
water for about 3 minutes until al dente, then drain.

Meanwhile, heat a wok or large frying pan until hot
and add a drizzle of oil. Tip in the prawn mixture and
the spring onions and stir-fry over a high heat for
2–3 minutes until the prawns are lightly browned.
Add the lemon juice and basil and stir well.

Serve the prawns immediately with the cooked pasta.

For spicy Asian prawns with jasmine rice, combine
the oil, garlic and chilli as above with the grated rind of
1 lime and 2 teaspoons grated fresh root ginger. Add
the prawns and stir well. Leave to marinate as above.
Put 150 g (5 oz) jasmine rice in a small saucepan,
cover with 300 ml (½ pint) cold water and add a little
salt. Bring to the boil, then reduce the heat, cover with
a tight-fitting lid and simmer over a very low heat for
12 minutes. Remove from the heat and leave to stand
for 10 minutes. Meanwhile, stir-fry the prawns and
spring onions as above, but add 1 tablespoon light
soy sauce just before the prawns are cooked. Add the
juice of the lime and 2 tablespoons chopped fresh
coriander and stir well. Fluff up the rice and serve with
the prawn mixture.

pasta, rice & noodles

creamy tuna & leek pasta

Serves **4**
Preparation time **10 minutes**
Cooking time **12 minutes**

400 g (13 oz) **dried penne**
2 tablespoons **extra virgin olive oil**
2 **leeks**, sliced
2 large **garlic cloves**, sliced
2 x 200 g (7 oz) cans **tuna in olive oil**, drained
150 ml (¼ pint) **dry white wine**
150 ml (¼ pint) **double cream**
2 tablespoons chopped **parsley**
salt and **black pepper**

Plunge the pasta into a large saucepan of lightly salted boiling water. Return to the boil and cook for 10–12 minutes until al dente. Drain well and return to the pan.

Meanwhile, heat the oil in a frying pan, add the leeks, garlic and salt and pepper to taste and cook gently for 5 minutes.

Flake in the tuna and cook, stirring, for 1 minute. Add the wine, bring to the boil and boil until reduced by half. Stir in the cream and heat through for 2–3 minutes.

Add the tuna sauce to the pasta with the parsley and stir over a medium heat for 1 minute. Serve immediately with a rocket salad.

For chicken, leek & rocket pasta, while the pasta is cooking as above, heat 4 tablespoons extra virgin olive oil in a frying pan, add 2 sliced leeks, 2 crushed garlic cloves and 2 deseeded and sliced red chillies and cook gently for 5 minutes. Add 250 g (8 oz) diced skinless chicken breast fillets and cook over a medium-high heat for about 5 minutes, or until golden and cooked through. Stir into the cooked, drained pasta with 150 g (5 oz) rocket leaves, a squeeze of lemon juice and a little extra oil. Serve immediately.

sausage meatballs, peas & pasta

Serves **4**
Preparation time **20 minutes**
Cooking time **15 minutes**

500 g (1 lb) **beef** or **pork
  sausages**, skins removed
4 tablespoons **extra virgin
  olive oil**
2 **garlic cloves**, sliced
2 tablespoons chopped
  sage
½ teaspoon **dried chilli flakes**
400 g (13 oz) **dried fusilli**
250 g (8 oz) **frozen peas**,
  thawed
salt and **black pepper**
freshly grated **Parmesan
  cheese**, to serve

Cut the sausagemeat into small pieces and roll into walnut-sized meatballs.

Heat half the oil in a large nonstick frying pan, add the meatballs and cook over a medium heat, stirring frequently, for 10 minutes until cooked through. Remove from the pan with a slotted spoon.

Meanwhile, plunge the pasta into a large saucepan of lightly salted boiling water. Return to the boil and cook for 8 minutes. Add the peas, return to the boil and cook for a further 2 minutes until the peas are just tender and the pasta is al dente. Drain well, reserving 4 tablespoons of the cooking water.

Add the garlic, sage, chilli flakes and salt and pepper to taste to the meatball pan and cook over a low heat for 2–3 minutes until the garlic is soft but not browned. Return the meatballs to the pan.

Return the pasta and peas to the pan and stir in the meatball mixture, reserved cooking water and remaining oil and heat through for 2 minutes. Serve in bowls topped with grated Parmesan.

For prawns, chorizo, peas & pasta, cook the pasta and peas as above. Meanwhile heat a dry frying pan until hot, add 150 g (5 oz) diced chorizo and fry over high heat for 3–4 minutes until the fat is released. Lower the heat, add 350 g (12 oz) peeled raw prawns and 2 crushed garlic cloves and stir-fry over a low heat for 5 minutes until the prawns are cooked. Stir this into the drained pasta and peas along with 4 tablespoons chopped fresh mint, juice of ½ lemon and a drizzle of extra virgin olive oil. Season to taste and serve.

macaroni cheese with chorizo

Serves **4**
Preparation time **5 minutes**
Cooking time **30 minutes**

250 g (8 oz) **dried macaroni**
125 g (4 oz) **chorizo**, diced
1 small **onion**, finely
  chopped
1 **garlic clove**, crushed
300 ml (10 fl oz) **double
  cream**
150 ml (5 fl oz) **chicken
  stock** (see page 44 for
  homemade)
75 g (3 oz) **Cheddar cheese**,
  grated
4 tablespoons freshly grated
  Parmesan cheese
salt and **black pepper**

Plunge the pasta into a saucepan of lightly salted boiling water. Return to the boil and simmer for 10–12 minutes until al dente. Drain well and return to the pan.

Meanwhile, heat a dry frying pan until hot, add the chorizo and cook for 3 minutes until browned and the fat is released. Remove from the pan with a slotted spoon. Add the onion and garlic to the pan and cook gently for 5 minutes until soft.

Stir in the macaroni with the chorizo, cream, stock and a little salt and pepper. Heat gently, stirring, for 2–3 minutes until warmed through. Stir in the Cheddar, remove the pan from the heat and stir until the cheese has melted.

Spoon the mixture into 4 x 300 ml (½ pint) baking dishes, sprinkle over the Parmesan and bake in a preheated oven, 190°C (375°F), Gas Mark 5, for 12–15 minutes until bubbling and golden. Serve with a crisp green salad.

For cheesy baked pasta with bacon, cook 250 g (8 oz) dried penne until al dente instead of the macaroni, and cook 125 g (4 oz) diced smoked bacon in place of the chorizo as above. Cook the onion and garlic as above, then stir in the penne, cream and salt and pepper and heat through for 2–3 minutes. Stir in 75 g (3 oz) grated Gruyère cheese, remove from the heat and stir until melted. Spoon the pasta mixture into a 1 litre (1¾ pint) baking dish, sprinkle with the Parmesan and bake in a preheated oven, 190°C (375°F), Gas Mark 5, for 25 minutes.

singapore chicken noodles

Serves **4**
Preparation time **10 minutes**,
   plus marinating
Cooking time **5–6 minutes**

350 g (12 oz) **skinless
   chicken thigh fillets**, sliced
2 tablespoons **light soy
   sauce**
1 tablespoon **caster sugar**
1 teaspoon **sesame oil**
2 tablespoons **oyster sauce**
2 tablespoons **rice wine
   vinegar**
3 tablespoons **vegetable oil**
4 **spring onions**, thickly
   sliced
2 **garlic cloves**, sliced
1 teaspoon grated **fresh root
   ginger**
350 g (12 oz) **fresh hokkein
   noodles**
50 g (2 oz) **bean sprouts**
sliced **red chillies**, to garnish

Put the chicken in a bowl. Add the soy sauce, sugar
and sesame oil and stir well. Cover and leave to
marinate at cool room temperature for 15 minutes.

Strain the chicken and reserve the marinade. Add
the oyster sauce and rice wine vinegar to the marinade
and set aside.

Heat half the vegetable oil in a wok or large frying pan
until starting to smoke. Add the chicken and stir-fry
over a high heat for 2–3 minutes until lightly golden.
Remove from the pan with a slotted spoon.

Heat the remaining oil in the pan, add the spring
onions, garlic and ginger and stir-fry over a high heat
for 1 minute. Return the chicken to the pan with the
noodles and marinade mixture and toss for 2 minutes
until heated through.

Stir through the bean sprouts and serve in bowls,
garnished with red chilli slices.

For barbecued Asian chicken, put the chicken slices
in a bowl and add 2 tablespoons light soy sauce,
½ teaspoon sesame oil, 1 tablespoon oyster sauce
and 1 teaspoon clear honey. Stir well until the chicken
is evenly coated. Thread on to metal skewers and
cook under a preheated high grill or on a preheated
hot barbecue or for 4–5 minutes on each side. Serve
with a salad.

pad thai

Serves **2**
Preparation time **10 minutes**
Cooking time **12 minutes**

250 g (8 oz) **dried rice noodles**
1½ tablespoons **sweet soy sauce**
1½ tablespoons **lime juice**
1 tablespoons **Thai fish sauce**
1 tablespoon **water**
3 tablespoons **groundnut oil**
2 **garlic cloves**, sliced
1 small **red chilli**, deseeded and chopped
125 g (4 oz) **firm tofu**, diced
2 **eggs**, lightly beaten
125 g (4 oz) **bean sprouts**
1 tablespoon chopped **fresh coriander**
4 tablespoons **salted peanuts**, chopped

Cook the noodles in boiling water for 5 minutes until softened. Drain and immediately refresh under cold water, drain again and set aside.

Combine the soy sauce, lime juice, fish sauce and measurement water in a small bowl and set aside.

Heat the oil in a wok or large frying pan, add the garlic and chilli and stir-fry over a medium heat for 30 seconds. Add the noodles and tofu and stir-fry for 2–3 minutes until heated through.

Carefully push the noodle mixture up the side of the pan, clearing the centre of the pan. Add the eggs and heat gently for 1 minute without stirring, then gently start 'scrambling' the eggs with a spoon. Mix the noodles back into the centre and stir well until mixed with the eggs.

Add the soy sauce mixture and cook for 1 minute, or until heated through. Stir in the bean sprouts and coriander. Spoon into bowls and serve immediately, topped with the peanuts.

For fresh noodle salad, cook 250 g (8 oz) dried rice noodles as above. Put in a bowl and add 1 shredded carrot, ½ sliced cucumber, 1 handful of bean sprouts and 1 handful each of basil, mint and fresh coriander leaves. Combine 1 teaspoon sesame oil, 2 tablespoons olive oil, 1 tablespoon Thai fish sauce, 2 teaspoons caster sugar and 1 tablespoon lime juice. Stir into the salad and serve garnished with 4 tablespoons chopped toasted peanuts.

sweet & sour pork noodles

Serves **2**
Preparation time **10 minutes**,
plus marinating
Cooking time **6–7 minutes**

250 g (8 oz) **pork fillet**
3 tablespoons **light soy
sauce**
2 tablespoons **sweet chilli
sauce**
1 tablespoon **caster sugar**
1 tablespoon **rice wine
vinegar**
3 tablespoons **vegetable oil**
2 **garlic cloves**, sliced
2 teaspoons grated **fresh
root ginger**
1 small **onion**, sliced
1 **red pepper**, cored,
deseeded and sliced
250 g (8 oz) **fresh hokkein
noodles**

Cut the pork into thin slices and put in a bowl.
Combine the soy and chilli sauces, sugar and vinegar
and add to the pork. Stir well until the pork is evenly
coated, cover and leave to marinate at cool room
temperature for 15 minutes. Strain the pork, reserve
the marinade and set aside.

Heat half the oil in a wok or large frying pan until
starting to smoke. Add the pork and stir-fry over a high
heat for 3–4 minutes until golden. Remove from the
pan with a slotted spoon.

Heat the remaining oil in the pan, add the garlic, ginger,
onion and red pepper and stir-fry over a high heat for
1 minute. Return the pork to the pan with the noodles
and marinade and toss for 2 minutes until heated
through. Serve immediately.

For chicken with plum sauce & noodles, thinly
slice 250 g (8 oz) skinless chicken breast fillets and
put in a bowl. Combine 1 tablespoon light soy sauce,
2 tablespoons plum sauce and the juice of ½ lime and
add to the chicken. Stir well until the chicken is evenly
coated, cover and leave to marinate at cool room
temperature for 15 minutes. Use as for the pork
above, but replace the red pepper with 125 g (4 oz)
broccoli florets. Serve the chicken and noodles
garnished with fresh coriander leaves.

everything rice

Serves **6**
Preparation time **20 minutes**
Cooking time **45–50 minutes**

1 kg (2 lb) **chicken**, jointed
  into 12 pieces (ask your
  butcher)
1 tablespoon **jerk seasoning**
4 tablespoons **olive oil**
1 **onion**, chopped
1 **red pepper**, cored,
  deseeded and chopped
2 **celery sticks**, chopped
2 **garlic cloves**, crushed
1 tablespoon chopped
  thyme
250 g (8 oz) **long-grain rice**
600 ml (1 pint) hot **chicken
  stock** (see page 44 for
  homemade)
250 g (8 oz) **piece of
  cooked ham**, diced
250 g (8 oz) **raw peeled
  prawns**
2 tablespoons chopped
  fresh coriander

Put the chicken pieces in a bowl, add the jerk
seasoning and salt and pepper and stir well to evenly
coat the chicken.

Heat the oil in a large frying pan, add the chicken
pieces and cook for 5–6 minutes until browned all over.
Remove from the pan with a slotted spoon.

Add the onion, red pepper, celery, garlic, thyme and salt
and pepper to taste to the pan and cook, stirring
frequently, for 10 minutes until golden. Return the
chicken to the pan.

Add the rice and stir well, then add the hot stock. Bring
to the boil, then reduce the heat, cover and simmer
gently for 20 minutes.

Stir in the ham and prawns and cook, covered, for a
further 10 minutes until the rice is tender and all the
stock has been absorbed. Adjust the seasoning and
serve immediately.

For classic paella, prepare and cook the chicken
and vegetables as above. After returning the chicken
to the pan, add 250 g (8 oz) paella rice and stir well.
Add the hot stock with 400 g (13 oz) can chopped
tomatoes. Bring to the boil, then reduce the heat,
cover and simmer gently for 35–40 minutes until
the rice is creamy and tender and most of the stock
has been absorbed. Adjust the seasoning and
serve immediately.

pea & prawn risotto

Serves **6**
Preparation time **10 minutes**
Cooking time **40 minutes**

500 g (1 lb) **raw prawns in their shells**
125 g (4 oz) **butter**
1 **onion**, finely chopped
2 **garlic cloves**, crushed
250 g (8 oz) **risotto rice**
375 g (12 oz) **fresh peas**
150 ml (¼ pint) **dry white wine**
1.5 litres (2½ pints) hot **vegetable stock** (see page 58 for homemade)
4 tablespoons chopped **mint**
salt and **black pepper**

Peel the prawns, reserving the heads and shells.

Melt 100 g (3½ oz) butter in a large frying pan and fry the prawn heads and shells for 3–4 minutes. Strain and return butter to the pan, discarding heads and shells.

Add the onion and garlic and cook for 5 minutes until softened but not coloured. Add the rice and stir well to coat the grains with the butter. Add the peas, then pour in the wine. Bring to the boil and cook, stirring, until reduced by half.

Add the hot stock, a large ladleful at a time, and cook, stirring constantly until each addition has been absorbed before adding the next. Continue in this way until all the stock has been absorbed and the rice is creamy but the grains are still firm. This should take about 20 minutes.

Melt the remaining butter in a separate frying pan, add the prawns and cook, stirring, for 3–4 minutes. Stir into the rice with the pan juices and mint and season to taste with salt and pepper.

For pea & prawn risotto cakes, cook the risotto as above, then leave to go cold. Stir in 2 beaten eggs and 50 g (2 oz) grated Parmesan cheese. Using damp hands, shape the mixture into 10 cm (4 inch) patties. Heat a shallow depth of vegetable oil in a frying pan, add the cakes, in batches, and cook for 3–4 minutes on each side until golden brown and heated through. Remove from the pan with a slotted spoon and keep warm in a preheated oven, 150°C (300°F), Gas Mark 2, while you cook the remainder. Serve with a crisp green salad.

baked risotto with burnt butter

Serves **4–6**
Preparation time **5 minutes**
Cooking time **40 minutes**

spray olive oil, for oiling
375 g (12 oz) **risotto rice**
1.2 litres (2 pints) hot
  chicken stock (see page
  44 for homemade)
50 g (2 oz) **butter**
50 g (2 oz) **Parmesan
  cheese**, freshly grated
salt and **black pepper**

Spray a 2 litre (3½ pint) casserole lightly with spray oil. Put the rice in the prepared dish and pour over the stock. Add a little salt and pepper, stir once and cover with a tight-fitting lid (add a layer of foil if necessary).

Bake in a preheated oven, 180°C (350°F), Gas Mark 4, for 40 minutes until the rice is tender and most of the stock has been absorbed.

Meanwhile, melt the butter in a small saucepan and cook gently for 2–3 minutes until the butter browns to a nutty colour.

Remove the risotto from the oven and stir in the Parmesan and the browned butter. Serve immediately.

For baked pumpkin risotto, combine 500 g (1 lb) peeled, deseeded and diced pumpkin in a roasting tin with 1 thinly sliced onion, 1 crushed garlic clove, 1 tablespoon chopped sage, 2 tablespoons extra virgin olive oil and salt and pepper to taste. Prepare the rice ready for baking as above and put in the oven, with the pumpkin mixture on the shelf below the risotto. After baking for 40 minutes, stir the pumpkin mixture and 50 g (2 oz) freshly grated Parmesan cheese into the baked risotto, then the browned butter as above.

meat, poultry & fish

herb & bacon chicken roast

Serves **4**
Preparation time **10 minutes**
Cooking time **45 minutes**

2 tablespoons **extra virgin
 olive oil**
2 tablespoons chopped
 thyme
2 **garlic cloves**, crushed
grated **rind** and **juice** of
 1 **lemon**
4 **chicken quarters**, about
 375 g (12 oz) each
4 **streaky bacon rashers**,
 rind removed
1 tablespoon **plain flour**
150 ml (¼ pint) **dry white
 wine**
300 ml (½ pint) **chicken
 stock** (see page 44 for
 homemade)
salt and **black pepper**

Combine the oil, thyme, garlic, lemon rind and salt and
pepper to taste in a bowl. Score the chicken quarters
several times with a sharp knife and rub all over with
the oil and herb mixture. Wrap each chicken quarter
with bacon using cocktail sticks to secure in place.

Transfer to a roasting tin and roast in a preheated
oven, 200°C (400°F), Gas Mark 6, for 35–40 minutes
until crisp and golden. Remove from the oven, transfer
the chicken pieces to a warm platter and wrap with foil.

Pour off all but 2 tablespoons fat from the roasting tin
and place the tin over a medium heat. Add the flour
and cook, stirring constantly, for 30 seconds. Gradually
whisk in the wine and then the stock and simmer for
5 minutes until thickened. Serve with the chicken.

For perfect roast potatoes to serve with the
chicken, cook 750 g (1½ lb) peeled potatoes in a
large saucepan of lightly salted boiling water for
10 minutes. Drain well, return to the pan and shake
firmly to fluff up the edges. Put 4 tablespoons olive oil
in a roasting tin and heat in a preheated oven, 200°C
(400°F), Gas Mark 6, for 5 minutes. Carefully tip in
the potatoes (the oil will spit) and roast in the oven
for 45–50 minutes, stirring halfway through, until crisp
and golden.

chicken with red wine & grapes

Serves **4**
Preparation time **5 minutes**
Cooking time **30 minutes**

3 tablespoons **olive oil**
4 **skinless chicken breast
   fillets**, about 150 g (5 oz)
   each
1 **red onion**, sliced
2 tablespoons **red pesto**
   (see below for homemade)
300 ml (½ pint) **red wine**
300 ml (½ pint) **water**
125 g (4 oz) **red grapes**,
   halved and deseeded
salt and **black pepper**
basil leaves, to garnish

Heat 2 tablespoons of the oil in a large frying pan, add the chicken breasts and cook over a medium heat for 5 minutes, turning frequently, until browned all over. Remove from the pan with a slotted spoon and drain on kitchen paper.

Heat the remaining oil in the pan, add the onion slices and pesto and cook, stirring constantly, for 3 minutes until the onion is softened but not browned.

Add the wine and measurement water to the pan and bring to the boil. Return the chicken breasts to the pan and season with salt and pepper to taste. Reduce the heat and simmer for 15 minutes, or until the chicken is cooked through.

Stir in the grapes and serve immediately, garnished with basil leaves.

For homemade red pesto, put 1 chopped garlic clove, ½ teaspoon sea salt, 25 g (1 oz) basil leaves, 50 g (2 oz) drained sun-dried tomatoes in oil, 125 ml (4 fl oz) extra virgin olive oil and a little pepper in a food processor or blender and blend until smooth. Transfer to a bowl and stir in 2 tablespoons freshly grated Parmesan cheese.

chicken thighs with fresh pesto

Serves **4**
Preparation time **10 minutes**
Cooking time **25 minutes**

1 tablespoon **olive oil**
8 **chicken thighs**

Green pesto
6 tablespoons **olive oil**
50 g (2 oz) **pine nuts**,
  toasted
50 g (2 oz) **Parmesan
  cheese**, freshly grated
50 g (2 oz) **basil leaves**,
  plus extra to garnish
15 g (½ oz) **flat leaf parsley**
2 **garlic cloves**, chopped
salt and **black pepper**

Heat the oil in a nonstick frying pan, add the chicken thighs and cook over a medium heat, turning frequently, for about 20 minutes or until the chicken is cooked through.

Meanwhile, make the pesto. Put all the ingredients in a food processor or blender and process until smooth.

Remove the chicken from the pan and keep hot. Reduce the heat and add the pesto to the pan. Heat through, stirring, for 2–3 minutes.

Pour the warmed pesto over the chicken thighs, garnish with basil and serve with steamed vegetables and roasted cherry tomatoes.

For chicken thighs with mustard & crème fraîche sauce, cook the chicken thighs as above, remove from the frying pan and keep warm. Reduce the heat, add 50 ml (2 fl oz) dry white wine and scrape the base of the pan to loosen the residue. Simmer until reduced by half. Stir in 125 g (4 oz) crème fraîche and 1 tablespoon wholegrain mustard and heat through, stirring, for 3 minutes. Pour over the chicken and serve garnished with chopped fresh chives.

chicken satay

Serves **6**
Preparation time **10 minutes**,
  plus marinating
Cooking time **10 minutes**

25 g (1 oz) **smooth peanut
  butter**
125 ml (4 fl oz) **soy sauce**
125 ml (4 fl oz) **lime juice**
15 g (½ oz) **curry powder**
2 **garlic cloves**, chopped
1 teaspoon **hot pepper
  sauce**
6 **skinless chicken breast
  fillets**, cubed

Combine the peanut butter, soy sauce, lime juice, curry powder, garlic and hot pepper sauce in a large non-metallic bowl.

Add the chicken to the marinade and stir well until evenly coated. Cover and leave to marinate in the refrigerator for about 12 hours or overnight.

When ready to cook, thread the chicken on to metal skewers and cook under a preheated high grill for 5 minutes on each side, or until cooked through. Serve immediately.

For piri piri chicken skewers, combine 4 tablespoons extra virgin olive oil, 2 chopped red chillies (deseeded if wished), 2 crushed garlic cloves and salt and pepper to taste in a large bowl. Reserve half the mixture separately, then add the chicken to the remaining half in the bowl and stir well until evenly coated. Cover and leave to marinate in the refrigerator for about 12 hours or overnight. Thread the chicken on to bamboo skewers, presoaked in boiling water for 10 minutes, and cook under a preheated high grill for 5 minutes on each side, or until cooked through. Serve drizzled with the remaining piri piri and a squeeze of lemon juice.

duck breasts with lentils

Serves **4**
Preparation time **10 minutes**
Cooking time **25–30 minutes**

4 x **Barbary duck breasts**,
   about 175 g (6 oz) each
175 g (6 oz) **Puy lentils**
150 ml (¼ pint) **chicken
   stock** (see page 44 for
   homemade)
salt and **black pepper**
chervil sprigs, to garnish

Marmalade
300 ml (½ pint) **orange juice**
250 g (8 oz) **mandarins**,
   pips removed but with peel
   left on, finely chopped

Sauce
3 **shallots**, finely chopped
50 ml (2 fl oz) **port**
150 ml (¼ pint) **red grape
   juice**

Put the duck breasts in a shallow roasting tray, skin side up, and roast in a preheated oven, 200°C (400°F), Gas 6, for 10–15 minutes – they should still be pink in the centre. Leave to rest for 5 minutes.

Meanwhile, put the lentils in a saucepan of salted water, bring to the boil and boil for 15 minutes, then drain.

While the duck and lentils are cooking, make the marmalade. Put the orange juice and mandarins in a stainless-steel saucepan. Bring to the boil, then reduce the heat and cook for 10 minutes, or until reduced by two-thirds. At the same time, for the sauce, heat a dry nonstick frying pan, add the shallots and cook gently for 2–3 minutes. Add the port and grape juice. Bring to the boil and boil for 10 minutes, or until reduced by half.

Remove the duck from the pan and set aside. Skim off the excess fat from the pan. Add the cooked lentils and stock and cook over a medium heat, scraping any residue from the pan, for 2–3 minutes until the stock has nearly all evaporated.

Slice the duck breasts. Divide the lentils between warmed plates and top with the duck slices. Spoon a little marmalade over the meat, pour the sauce around the lentils and serve garnished with chervil sprigs.

lamb rogan josh

Serves **4**
Preparation time **20 minutes**,
plus marinating
Cooking time **2 hours**

1 kg (2 lb) **boneless leg of
lamb**
400 g (13 oz) can **chopped
tomatoes**
300 ml (½ pint) **water**
1 teaspoon **caster sugar**
2 tablespoons chopped
fresh coriander, plus extra
to garnish

Marinade
1 **onion**, roughly chopped
4 **garlic cloves**, roughly
chopped
2 teaspoon grated **fresh root
ginger**
1 large **red chilli**, chopped
2 teaspoons **ground coriander**
1½ teaspoon **salt**
1 teaspoon **ground cumin**
1 teaspoon **ground turmeric**
½ teaspoon **ground cinnamon**
½ teaspoon **ground white
pepper**
2 tablespoons **red wine
vinegar**

Cut the lamb into chunks, discarding any gristle, and put in a large non-metallic bowl.

Make the marinade. Put all the ingredients in a food processor or blender and process to a smooth paste. Add to the lamb and stir well until evenly coated. Cover and leave to marinate in the refrigerator overnight.

When ready to cook, put the meat and all the marinade juices in a saucepan with the tomatoes, measurement water and sugar. Bring to the boil, then reduce the heat cover and simmer gently for 1½ hours.

Stir in the fresh coriander and cook, uncovered, for a further 25–30 minutes until the sauce is thickened. Adjust the seasoning, garnish with the coriander and serve with rice (see below).

For perfect rice to serve with the curry, put 300 g (10 oz) basmati rice in a large saucepan with 1.5 litres (2½ pints) cold water and 1 teaspoon salt. Bring to the boil, then reduce the heat and simmer for 10 minutes. Drain the rice in a sieve and then place the sieve back over the pan. Cover the whole sieve and pan with a clean tea towel and leave to stand for 5 minutes. Fluff up the grains with a fork and serve.

lamb & courgette koftas

Serves **4**
Preparation time **20 minutes**
Cooking time **20 minutes**

2 **courgettes**, finely grated
2 tablespoons **sesame seeds**
250 g (8 oz) **minced lamb**
2 **spring onions**, finely chopped
1 **garlic clove**, crushed
1 tablespoon chopped **mint**
½ teaspoon **ground mixed spice**
2 tablespoons **dried breadcrumbs**
1 **egg**, lightly beaten
vegetable oil, for shallow-frying
salt and **black pepper**
lemon wedges, to garnish

Put the courgettes in a sieve and press down to extract as much liquid as possible. Transfer to a bowl.

Heat a dry heavy-based frying pan until hot, add the sesame seeds and cook, shaking constantly, for 1–2 minutes until golden brown and aromatic. Add to the courgettes, together with the lamb and all the remaining ingredients, except the oil and lemon wedges. Season liberally with salt and pepper.

Form the mixture into 20 small balls. Heat a shallow depth of oil in a frying pan, add the koftas, in batches, and cook for 5 minutes, turning frequently until evenly browned. Keep the cooked koftas warm in a preheated oven, 160°C (325°F), Gas Mark 3, while you cook the remainder. Serve hot, garnished with lemon wedges.

For tahini sauce to serve as an accompaniment, combine 250 ml (8 fl oz) Greek yogurt, 2 crushed garlic cloves, 1 tablespoon tahini paste, 2 teaspoons lemon juice and salt and pepper to taste in a bowl.

mustard lamb fillet

Serves **4**
Preparation time **10 minutes**,
  plus resting
Cooking time **10–15 minutes**

500 g (1 lb) **neck fillet of
  lamb**
4 **garlic cloves**, crushed
2 tablespoon **Dijon** or
  English mustard
2 tablespoons chopped **mint**
1 tablespoon chopped **fresh
  coriander**
1 tablespoon **olive oil**

Trim the lamb of any fat.

Combine the garlic, mustard, mint, coriander and oil in
a small bowl.

Rub the lamb with the garlic and mustard mixture.
Transfer to a baking dish.

Bake in a preheated oven, 200°C (400°F), Gas 6, for
10–15 minutes, or until the lamb is cooked to your
liking. Leave to rest for 10 minutes, then serve with a
selection of steamed vegetables.

For sweet potato mash to serve with the lamb, cook
500 g (1 lb) peeled sweet potatoes with 375 g (12 oz)
peeled potatoes in a large saucepan of lightly salted
boiling water until tender. Drain well and return to the
pan. Mash in 50 g (2 oz) butter, 50 ml (2 fl oz) milk
and salt and pepper to taste.

pork spare ribs

Serve **4**
Preparation time **5 minutes**
Cooking time **1 hour**

2 **pork spare rib racks**
   (about 1 kg (2 lb) each)
100 ml (3½ fl oz) **tomato**
   ketchup
2 tablespoons **clear honey**
1 tablespoon **dark soy sauce**
1 tablespoon **olive oil**
1 tablespoon **malt vinegar**
2 teaspoons **Dijon mustard**
salt and **black pepper**

Arrange the ribs on a wire rack in a large roasting tin. Combine the remaining ingredients in a bowl. Brush the ribs generously on both sides with the marinade.

Roast the ribs in a preheated oven, 200°C (400°F), Gas Mark 6, for 30 minutes.

Baste the ribs again on both sides with the marinade, using a clean brush, and roast for a further 30 minutes until golden and sticky.

Remove from the oven, brush over the remaining marinade and leave to cool for 5 minutes before serving, divided into 4 portions.

For Chinese hoisin wings, combine all the marinade ingredients in a bowl as above, but adding 2 tablespoons hoisin sauce. Mix with 12 large chicken wings to coat evenly. Roast the wings in a preheated oven, 200°C (400°F), Gas Mark 6, for 30–35 minutes until crisp and golden and cooked through.

marinated pork fillet

Serves **4**
Preparation time **10 minutes**,
  plus marinating
Cooking time **20 minutes**

2 **pork fillets**, about 250 g
  (8 oz) each
1 tablespoon **linseeds**
150 ml (¼ pint) **dry white
  wine**

Marinade
1 **cinnamon stick**
2 tablespoons **soy sauce**
2 **garlic cloves**, crushed
1 teaspoon grated **fresh root
  ginger**
1 tablespoon **clear honey**
1 teaspoon crushed
  coriander seeds
1 teaspoon **sesame oil**

Combine the marinade ingredients in a bowl. Put the pork fillets in a shallow dish and coat evenly with the marinade. Cover and leave to marinate in the refrigerator for at least 2–3 hours, and preferably overnight.

When ready to cook, drain the pork, reserving the marinade. Lay the pork in the linseeds on both sides so that it is evenly covered. Heat a baking sheet or roasting tin on the hob, add the pork and cook over a high heat until browned and sealed on both sides. Transfer to a preheated oven, 180°C (350°F), Gas Mark 4, and roast for 15 minutes, or until golden brown.

Meanwhile, remove the cinnamon stick from the marinade and pour the liquid into a nonstick saucepan. Add the wine and bring to the boil, then reduce the heat and simmer until it has the consistency of a sticky glaze. Remove the pan from the heat.

Cut the roasted pork into 5 mm (¼ inch) slices. Serve on a bed of steamed vegetables, such as pak choi or spinach, and drizzle the glaze over the pork.

For pork fillet with Dukhah crust, omit marinating the pork. Heat a dry frying pan until hot, then dry fry 25 g (1 oz) sesame seeds, 2 tablespoons coriander seeds and ½ tablespoon cumin seeds for 2 minutes until browned. Leave to cool, then grind in a spice grinder. Stir in 25 g (1 oz) toasted and chopped blanched almonds, ½ teaspoon salt and a little pepper. Transfer to a plate and press the pork fillets in the mixture to coat on both sides. Roast the pork on a baking sheet or in a roasting tin as above. Rest for 5 minutes, then serve with a green salad.

asparagus & prosciutto wraps

Serves **3**
Preparation time **10 minutes**
Cooking time **28 minutes**

18 thick **asparagus spears**,
  trimmed
250 g (8 oz) **mozzarella
  cheese**
250 g (8 oz) thinly sliced
  prosciutto
75 g (3 oz) **butter**, plus extra
  for greasing
black pepper

Plunge the asparagus into a large saucepan of salted boiling water, then cook over a medium heat for 4–8 minutes, or until just tender.

Drain and plunge into cold water. When cooled, drain again and set aside.

Cut the mozzarella into 18 equal slices. Separate the prosciutto slices into 6 even piles and cut the butter into 12 even-sized knobs.

Take 3 asparagus spears and put them on 1 bundle of prosciutto. Put 2 pieces of mozzarella in between the spears, along with a knob of butter. Wrap the prosciutto around the asparagus, using all the slices in the pile. Repeat until you have 6 bundles.

Lightly grease an ovenproof dish and arrange the asparagus bundles over the base. Put a slice of mozzarella and a knob of butter on each bundle. Season with pepper and bake at the top of a preheated oven, 200°C (400°F), Gas 6, for 20 minutes.

For asparagus with lemon & garlic butter sauce, cook the asparagus spears as above. Meanwhile, put 125 g (4 oz) butter, 1 crushed garlic clove, finely grated rind of 1 lemon and a little pepper in a saucepan and cook gently until the garlic is soft. Whisk in 1 tablespoon lemon juice and serve drizzled over the asparagus.

pork with savoy cabbage

Serves **4**
Preparation time **15 minutes**
Cooking time **40 minutes**

1 tablespoon **sesame seeds**
2 **garlic cloves**, very finely
  sliced
3 **spring onions**, diagonally
  sliced into 1.5 cm (¾ inch)
  pieces
½ teaspoon **cayenne pepper**
300 g (10 oz) **pork loin**, cut
  into thick strips
2 tablespoons **olive oil**
2 teaspoons **sesame oil**
2 tablespoons **soy sauce**
2 teaspoons **clear honey**
400 g (13 oz) **Savoy
  cabbage**, cut into strips

Heat a dry heavy-based frying pan until hot, add
the sesame seeds and cook, shaking constantly, for
1–2 minutes until golden brown and aromatic. Remove
to a cool plate and set aside.

Combine the garlic, spring onions and cayenne pepper
in a bowl. Add the pork and mix well.

Heat the oils in a frying pan, add the pork, in 3 batches,
and stir-fry over a high heat for 5 minutes on each side,
or until golden and cooked through. Remove from the
pan with a slotted spoon.

Add the soy sauce, honey and cabbage to the pan and
toss to mix. Cover and cook over a medium heat for
5–6 minutes.

Return the pork to the pan, add the sesame seeds and
toss well. Serve immediately.

For orange & mustard seed rice to serve with the
pork, put 250 g (8 oz) jasmine rice in a saucepan and
add 500 ml (17 fl oz) cold water and 1 teaspoon salt.
Bring to the boil, then reduce the heat, cover with a
tight-fitting lid and simmer over a very low heat for
12 minutes. Meanwhile, melt 25 g (1 oz) butter in a
small saucepan, add 1 tablespoon mustard seeds and
grated rind of 1 orange and cook gently, stirring, for
2–3 minutes until the mustard seeds turn golden.
Remove the rice from the heat, pour in the mustard
seed mixture and replace the lid. Leave to stand for
10 minutes, then stir well and serve.

thai chilli beef burgers

Serves **4**
Preparation time **10 minutes**
Cooking time **10–12 minutes**

500 g (1 lb) **minced beef**
1 tablespoon **Thai red curry paste**
25 g (1 oz) **fresh white breadcrumbs**
2 tablespoons chopped **fresh coriander**
1 **egg**, lightly beaten
1 tablespoon **light soy sauce**
black pepper

To serve
1 **French stick**, cut into 4 and split lengthways
shredded lettuce
sweet chilli sauce

Put the minced beef in a bowl and stir in the red curry paste, breadcrumbs, coriander, egg, soy sauce and pepper. Mix together thoroughly with your hands until sticky. Shape the mixture into 8 mini burgers.

Heat a ridged griddle pan until very hot, add the burgers and cook over a high heat for 4–5 minutes on each side until charred and cooked through.

Serve each burger in the French sticks with some shredded lettuce and sweet chilli sauce.

For beef satay burgers, prepare and cook the burgers as above. Make a satay sauce by combining 6 tablespoons coconut cream, 3 tablespoons peanut sauce, juice of ½ lime, 2 teaspoons Thai fish sauce and 2 teaspoons sweet chilli sauce in a saucepan. Heat gently, stirring, for 2–3 minutes until blended. Assemble the burgers in the toasted sesame seed buns with some salad leaves and the satay sauce.

shepherd's pie

Serves **4–6**
Preparation time **20 minutes**
Cooking time **1 hour
20 minutes–1 hour
25 minutes**

1 tablespoon **olive oil**
1 **onion**, finely chopped
1 **carrot**, diced
1 **celery stick**, diced
1 tablespoon chopped
  thyme
500 g (1 lb) **minced lamb**
400 g (13 oz) can **chopped
  tomatoes**
4 tablespoons **tomato purée**
750 g (1½ lb) **potatoes**, such
  as Desiree, peeled and
  cubed
50 g (2 oz) **butter**
3 tablespoons **milk**
75 g (3 oz) **Cheddar cheese**,
  grated
salt and **black pepper**

Heat the oil in a saucepan, add the onion, carrot, celery and thyme and cook gently for 10 minutes until soft and golden.

Add the minced lamb and cook over a high heat, breaking up with a wooden spoon, for 5 minutes until browned. Add the tomatoes, tomato purée and salt and pepper to taste. Bring to the boil, then reduce the heat, cover and simmer for 30 minutes.

Remove the lid and cook for a further 15 minutes until thickened.

Meanwhile, put the potatoes in a large saucepan of lightly salted water and bring to the boil. Reduce the heat and simmer for 15–20 minutes until really tender. Drain well and return to the pan. Mash in the butter, milk and half the cheese and season to taste with salt and pepper.

Spoon the minced lamb mixture into a 2 litre (3½ pint) baking dish and carefully spoon the mash over the top, spreading over the surface of the filling. Fork the top of the mash and scatter over the remaining cheese. Bake in a preheated oven, 190°C (375°F), Gas Mark 5, for 20–25 minutes until bubbling and golden.

For curried lamb filo pies, prepare and cook the minced meat mixture as above, adding 1 tablespoon medium curry paste with the tomatoes, tomato purée and seasoning. Spoon the filling into 6 x 300 ml (½ pint) ovenproof dishes. Layer 4 sheets of filo pastry together, brushing each with melted butter. Cut into 6 and scrunch each over a dish to cover. Bake in a preheated oven, 190°C (375°F), Gas Mark 5, for 20 minutes.

chilli tacos

Serves **4**
Preparation time **15 minutes**
Cooking time **25 minutes**

2 tablespoons **olive oil**
1 large **onion**, finely
  chopped
2 **garlic cloves**, crushed
500 g (1 lb) **lean minced
  beef**
700 g (1 lb 7 oz) jar **passata**
400 g (13 oz) can **red
  kidney beans**, drained
2–3 tablespoon **hot chilli
  sauce**
8 **soft corn tortillas**
125 g (4 oz) **Cheddar
  cheese**, grated
125 g (4 oz) **soured cream**
handful **fresh coriander
  sprigs**
salt and **black pepper**

Heat the oil in a saucepan, add the onion and garlic and cook over a high heat for 5 minutes.

Add the minced beef and cook, breaking it up with a wooden spoon, for 5 minutes until browned. Stir in the passata, beans, chilli sauce and salt and pepper to taste and bring to the boil. Reduce the heat and simmer, uncovered, for 15 minutes until thickened.

Meanwhile, put the corn tortillas on a large baking sheet and heat in a preheated oven, 180°C (350°F), Gas Mark 4, for 5 minutes.

Serve the tortillas on a platter in the centre of the table. Take 2 tortillas per person and spoon some chilli into each one. Top with a quarter of the cheese and soured cream and a little coriander, roll up and serve.

For lentil & red pepper chilli, heat 2 tablespoons olive oil in a saucepan, add 1 finely chopped large onion, 1 large cored, deseeded and chopped red pepper and 2 crushed garlic cloves and cook over a high heat for 5 minutes. Add 2 x 400 g (13 oz) cans brown lentils, drained, together with the passata, beans, chilli sauce and salt and pepper to taste as above. Bring to the boil, then reduce the heat and simmer, uncovered, for 15 minutes. Meanwhile, cook 300 g (10 oz) basmati rice in a large saucepan of salted boiling water for 10–12 minutes until just tender, then drain. Serve the chilli hot with the rice, guacamole (see page 26 for homemade) and soured cream.

swordfish brochettes & lemon rice

Serves **4**
Preparation time **10 minutes**,
  plus standing
Cooking time **20 minutes**

3 tablespoons **extra virgin
  olive oil**
1 large **onion**, finely chopped
2 teaspoons **ground turmeric**
1 teaspoon **ground cinnamon**
grated **rind** and **juice** of
  1 lemon
300 g (10 oz) **jasmine rice**
750 ml (1¼ pints) **chicken
  stock** (see page 44 for
  homemade)
750 g (1½ lb) **swordfish
  steaks**, cut into 2.5 cm
  (1 inch) dice
2 tablespoons chopped
  fresh coriander
salt and **black pepper**
spray oil for oiling

Heat 2 tablespoons of the oil in a saucepan, and add the onion, spices, lemon rind and salt and pepper to taste and cook gently for 5 minutes until softened.

Add the rice and stir well. Pour in the stock and bring to the boil. Reduce the heat, cover and simmer gently for 10 minutes. Stir in the lemon juice, remove the pan from the heat and leave to stand, covered, for 10 minutes. Stir in the coriander.

While the rice is standing, thread the swordfish cubes on to 8 bamboo skewers, presoaked in boiling water for 10 minutes. Brush with the remaining oil and season well with salt and pepper. Spray a preheated ridged grill pan with oil and cook the brochettes for 2 minutes on each side until evenly browned. Serve the rice and kebabs with a rocket salad, if liked.

For prawn, cranberry & cashew nut pilaf, prepare and cook the rice as above. After simmering gently for 10 minutes, stir in the juice of the lemon with 375 g (12 oz) cooked peeled prawns, 50 g (2 oz) toasted unsalted cashew nuts and 50 g (2 oz) dried cranberries. Leave to stand, covered, for 10 minutes before serving.

salmon with fennel & tomatoes

Serves **4**
Preparation time **10 minutes**
Cooking time **25 minutes**

4 **salmon fillets**, about
175–250 g (6–8 oz) each
4 tablespoons **lemon juice**
4 tablespoons **olive oil**
1 tablespoon **balsamic
vinegar**
1 tablespoon **clear honey**
4 **garlic cloves**, finely
chopped
2 **red onions**, quartered
2 **fennel bulbs**, quartered
16–20 **vine cherry tomatoes**
salt and **black pepper**

Season the salmon fillets generously with salt and
pepper and pour over the lemon juice. Set aside.

Combine the oil, vinegar, honey, garlic and salt and
pepper to taste in a small bowl. Put the onions, fennel
and tomatoes in a large bowl and pour over the oil
mixture. Toss to coat thoroughly, then spread out on a
baking sheet.

Roast in a preheated oven, 220°C (425°F), Gas Mark
7, for 10 minutes. Add the salmon fillets to the baking
sheet and roast for a further 12–15 minutes.

Serve the salmon with the roasted vegetables and rice
or couscous.

For lemon & herb couscous to serve with the
salmon and fennel, put 250 g (8 oz) couscous in a
heatproof bowl and pour over 250 ml (8 fl oz) boiling
vegetable stock (see page 58 for homemade). Cover
the bowl with a clean tea towel and leave to stand for
5 minutes, or until the grains are swollen and all the
liquid has been absorbed. Stir in 2 tablespoons extra
virgin olive oil, the juice of 1 lemon and 2 tablespoons
chopped mixed herbs, fluffing up the grains with a fork.

tuna fish cakes

Serves **4**
Preparation time **10 minutes**
Cooking time **20 minutes**

2 x 425 g (14 oz) cans **tuna
in olive oil**, drained
300 g (10 oz) **ricotta cheese**
6 **spring onions**, finely
chopped
grated **rind** and **juice** of
1 **lime**
1 tablespoon chopped **dill**
1 **egg**, beaten
3 tablespoons **extra virgin
olive oil**
100 g (3½ oz) **baby rocket
leaves**
salt and **black pepper**

Flake the tuna into a bowl and beat in the ricotta,
spring onions, lime rind, dill, egg and salt and pepper
to taste with a wooden spoon. Reserve 2 teaspoons
of the lime juice and beat the remainder into the
tuna mixture. Shape into 12 small cakes about 7 cm
(3 inches) across.

Heat half the oil in a frying pan, add the fish cakes,
in 2 batches, and cook over a medium heat for
4–5 minutes on each side until golden. Reduce the
heat if they start to over-brown and cook for a further
1 minute. Remove from the pan with a slotted spoon
and keep the cooked fish cakes warm in a preheated
oven, 160° (325°F), Gas Mark 3, while you cook
the remainder.

Meanwhile, whisk the remaining oil and lime juice
together and toss with the rocket leaves in a bowl.
Serve the fish cakes with the rocket salad and some
garlic & herb mayonnaise (see below).

For quick garlic & herb mayonnaise to serve with
the fish cakes, add 1 crushed garlic clove, 2 teaspoons
lime juice, 1 tablespoon chopped fresh coriander and a
pinch of cayenne pepper to 150 g (5 oz) good-quality
shop-bought mayonnaise in a bowl and mix well. Taste
and add more garlic according to taste.

warm scallop salad

Serves **4**
Preparation time **10 minutes**
Cooking time **3 minutes**

250 g (8 oz) **wild
  strawberries**, hulled
2 tablespoons **balsamic
  vinegar**
1 tablespoon **lemon juice**,
  plus juice of 1 **lemon**
50 ml (2 fl oz) **olive oil**
12 **king scallops**, without
  corals, cut into 3 slices
250 g (8 oz) **mixed salad
  leaves**
salt and **black pepper**

To garnish
1 tablespoon **olive oil**
3 **leeks**, cut into matchstick-
  thin strips
20 **wild strawberries** or 8
  larger strawberries, sliced

Put the strawberries, vinegar, 1 tablespoon lemon juice and oil in a food processor or blender and process until smooth. Pass through a fine sieve or muslin cloth to remove the pips and set aside.

Season the scallops with salt and pepper and the remaining lemon juice.

Prepare the garnish. Heat the oil in a nonstick frying pan, add the leeks and cook over a high heat, stirring, for 1 minute, or until golden brown. Remove and set aside.

Add the scallop slices to the pan and cook for 20–30 seconds on each side. Divide the salad leaves into quarters and pile in the centre of individual serving plates. Arrange the scallop slices over the salad.

Heat the strawberry mixture gently in a small saucepan for 20–30 seconds, then pour over the scallops and salad leaves. Scatter over the leeks and garnish with the strawberries. Sprinkle with a little pepper and serve.

For scallops with soy & honey dressing, whisk together 2 tablespoons extra virgin olive oil, 1 teaspoon sesame oil, 1 tablespoon light soy sauce, 2 teaspoons balsamic vinegar, 1 teaspoon clear honey and pepper to taste in a bowl. Cook the scallops as above (omitting the leeks) and arrange over the salad. Heat the dressing gently as above, then pour over the scallops and salad leaves.

fish 'n' oven chips

Serves **4**
Preparation time **10 minutes**
Cooking time **35–40 minutes**

4–6 large **potatoes**, such as
  Desiree, scrubbed
2 tablespoons **olive oil**, plus
  extra for shallow-frying
100 g (3½ oz) **dried
  breadcrumbs**
50 g (2 oz) **polenta**
1 tablespoon chopped
  thyme
4 **haddock** or **cod fillets**,
  about 175 g (6 oz) each
3 tablespoons **plain flour**,
  seasoned with salt and
  black pepper
2 **eggs**, lightly beaten
salt and **black pepper**
tomato ketchup, to serve

Cut the potatoes into wedges (you should get about
8–12 thick wedges from each potato). Toss with the oil
and salt and pepper to taste in a roasting tin and roast
in a preheated oven, 220°C (425°F), Gas Mark 7, for
35–40 minutes, turning once, until evenly browned.

Meanwhile, combine the breadcrumbs, polenta, thyme
and salt and pepper to taste in a large bowl. Dust each
fish fillet with seasoned flour and then dip into the
beaten egg and finally into the breadcrumb mixture to
completely coat the fish.

About 10 minutes before the chips are ready, heat
1 cm (½ inch) oil in a large frying pan, add the fish
fillets, in 2 batches, and cook over a medium heat for
2–3 minutes on each side until the coating is crisp and
golden and the fish is cooked through. Remove from the
pan with a fish slice and keep warm in the bottom of the
oven while you cook the remainder. Serve with the oven
chips and tomato ketchup.

For crispy-coated chicken niblets, cut 2 skinless
chicken breast fillets into strips about 2.5 cm (1 inch)
thick. Following the method above, dip the chicken
pieces into the seasoned flour, then the beaten egg
and finally the breadcrumb mixture to completely coat.
Shallow-fry as above, in 2 batches, for 4–5 minutes on
each side until crisp and golden. Serve with Quick
Garlic & Herb Mayonnaise (see page 158) for dipping.

parma ham-wrapped salmon

Serves **4**
Preparation time **10 minutes**
Cooking time **10 minutes**

4 **salmon fillets**, about 175 g
   (6 oz) each, skinned
4 thin slices of **fontina
   cheese**, rind removed
16 **sage leaves**
8 thin slices of **Parma ham**
salt and **black pepper**
rocket and parsley pasta,
   to serve (see below)

Season the salmon fillets with salt and pepper. Trim the slices of fontina to fit on top of the salmon.

Lay a slice of the trimmed cheese on top of each salmon fillet, followed by 4 sage leaves. Wrap 2 slices of Parma ham around each salmon fillet to hold the cheese and sage leaves in place.

Heat a griddle pan until hot, add the wrapped salmon fillets and cook for 5 minutes on each side, taking care when turning them over.

Serve the salmon hot with rocket and parsley pasta (see below).

For rocket & parsley pasta to serve as an accompaniment, plunge 375 g (12 oz) dried fusilli into a large saucepan of lightly salted boiling water, return to the boil and cook for 10–12 minutes until al dente. Drain well and return to the pan. Add 2 tablespoons extra virgin olive oil, 50 g (2 oz) baby rocket leaves, 2 tablespoons torn flat leaf parsley leaves and salt and pepper to taste and stir well.

easy fish pie

Serves **4**
Preparation time **15 minutes**
Cooking time **40 minutes**

75 g (3 oz) **butter**
1 small **onion**, finely chopped
1 **leek**, sliced
2 **celery sticks**, sliced
2 **garlic cloves**, crushed
grated **rind** of 1 **lemon**
2 teaspoons chopped
  tarragon
300 ml (½ pint) **double
  cream**
500 g (1 lb) **white fish fillets**,
  such as haddock, cod or
  plaice, cubed
150 g (5 oz) **raw peeled
  prawns**
1 small **baguette**, thinly
  sliced
salt and **black pepper**

Melt 25 g (1 oz) of the butter in a saucepan, add the
onion, leek, celery, garlic, lemon rind, tarragon and salt
and pepper to taste and cook gently for 10 minutes
until soft.

Add the cream and bring to the boil, then reduce the
heat and simmer gently for 2 minutes until thickened.
Remove from the heat and stir in the fish and prawns.

Spoon the seafood mixture into a 1 litre (1¾ pint) pie
dish. Melt the remaining butter in a small saucepan.
Arrange the bread slices over the fish, overlapping, and
brush with the melted butter.

Bake in a preheated oven, 180°C (350°F), Gas Mark 4,
for 15–20 minutes until the bread is golden. Cover
with foil and bake for a further 10 minutes until the
fish is cooked.

For curried prawn pies, after the onion and leek
mixture has been cooked for 10 minutes as above,
stir in 2 teaspoons mild curry powder and cook over a
medium heat, stirring constantly, for 2 minutes. Add the
cream and bring to the boil, then reduce the heat and
simmer gently for 2 minutes until thickened. Remove
the pan from the heat and stir in 125 g (4 oz) thawed
frozen peas with the fish and prawns. Spoon the
mixture into 4 individual baking dishes. Divide the bread
slices between the dishes, brush with the melted butter
and bake in the oven as above for 15 minutes.

prawns in chillied tomato sauce

Serves **4**
Preparation time **10 minutes**
Cooking time **10–12 minutes**

2 tablespoons **olive oil**
2 **red onions**, finely chopped
3 **garlic cloves**, crushed
1 **red chilli**, deseeded and
   chopped
2 strips of **lemon rind**
2 large **tomatoes**, deseeded
   and chopped
150 ml (¼ pint) **fish stock**
   (see below for homemade)
500 g (1 lb) **raw peeled**
   tiger prawns (heads, tails
   and shells reserved for
   making stock, optional)
salt and **black pepper**
2 tablespoons chopped
   mixed **parsley** and **dill**

Heat the oil in a heavy-based frying pan, add the onions, garlic, chilli and lemon rind and cook over a medium heat, stirring, for 1–2 minutes.

Add the tomatoes and stock to the pan and bring to the boil, then reduce the heat and simmer for 5 minutes.

Add the prawns, season to taste with salt and pepper and cook, turning occasionally, for about 4 minutes, or until the prawns turn pink.

Sprinkle with the mixed herbs and serve immediately.

For homemade fish stock, put the prawn heads, tails and shells in a mortar and lightly pound with a pestle. Put in a saucepan with the juice of ½ lemon and 150 ml (¼ pint) dry white wine and bring to the boil. Add 1.2 litres (2 pints) water, 1 diced onion, 1 garlic clove, peeled but left whole, 3–4 parsley stalks and 2–3 black peppercorns. Reduce the heat and simmer for about 15 minutes. Strain and use. This makes about 1 litre (1¾ pints) stock.

vegetarian
dishes &
salads

spring vegetable & herb pilaf

Serves **4**
Preparation time **10 minutes**,
  plus standing
Cooking time **20 minutes**

2 tablespoons **extra virgin
  olive oil**
1 **leek**, sliced
1 **courgette**, diced
grated **rind** and **juice** of
  1 **lemon**
2 **garlic cloves**, crushed
300 g (10 oz) **long-grain rice**
600 ml (1 pint) hot **vegetable
  stock** (see page 58 for
  homemade)
150 g (5 oz) **green beans**,
  chopped
150 g (5 oz) **fresh** or **frozen
  peas**
4 tablespoons chopped
  mixed herbs, such as mint,
  parsley and chives
50 g (2 oz) **flaked almonds**,
  toasted
salt and **black pepper**

Heat the oil in a large frying pan, add the leek,
courgette, lemon rind, garlic and a little salt and pepper
and cook gently over a medium-low heat for 5 minutes.

Add the rice, stir once and pour in the hot stock. Bring
to the boil, then reduce the heat, cover and simmer
gently for 10 minutes.

Stir in the beans and peas, cover and cook for a
further 5 minutes.

Remove the pan from the heat and leave to stand for
5 minutes. Stir in the lemon juice and herbs and serve
scattered with the flaked almonds.

For winter vegetable & fruit pilaf, heat
2 tablespoons extra virgin olive oil in a large frying
pan, add 1 sliced red onion, 1 teaspoon ground
coriander and 2 teaspoons chopped thyme and
cook gently over a medium-low heat for 5 minutes.
Add 375 g (12 oz) diced pumpkin flesh with the rice
as above, stir once and pour in the hot stock. Bring
to the boil, then reduce the heat, cover and simmer
gently for 10 minutes. Stir in 75 g (3 oz) raisins with
the peas as above, cover and cook for 5 minutes.
Remove the pan from the heat and leave to stand for
5 minutes. Stir in 2 tablespoons chopped fresh
coriander with the lemon juice and almonds.

spaghetti with easy tomato sauce

Serves **4**
Preparation time **5 minutes**
Cooking time **30 minutes**

400 g (13 oz) **dried
   spaghetti**
salt and **black pepper**
25 g (1 oz) freshly grated
   Parmesan cheese, to serve

Easy tomato sauce
2 x 400 g (13 oz) cans
   chopped tomatoes
2 tablespoons **extra virgin
   olive oil**
2 large **garlic cloves**,
   crushed
1 teaspoon **caster sugar**
¼ teaspoon **dried chilli flakes**
2 tablespoons chopped
   fresh basil

Start by making the sauce. Place the tomatoes, oil, garlic, sugar, chilli and some salt and pepper in a saucepan and bring to the boil. Lower the heat and simmer gently for 20–30 minutes until thickened and full of flavour.

Stir in the basil and adjust the seasoning. Keep warm.

Meanwhile, plunge the pasta into a saucepan of lightly salted, boiling water, bring back to the boil and cook for 10–12 minutes or until just tender. Drain the pasta and divide between bowls, spoon over the sauce and serve with Parmesan cheese.

For a spicy tomato & olive sauce, follow the recipe above but adding ½ teaspoon dried chilli flakes. Stir in 125 g (4 oz) pitted black olives just before the end of cooking and heat through.

aubergine & mozzarella bake

Serves **4**
Preparation time **15 minutes**,
 plus making the sauce
Cooking time **25–30 minutes**

spray olive oil, for oiling
2 large **aubergines**, about
 500 g (1 lb) each
3 tablespoons **extra virgin
 olive oil**
1 recipe quantity **Easy
 Tomato Sauce** (see page
 174)
250 g (8 oz) **mozzarella
 cheese**, grated
25 g (1 oz) **Parmesan
 cheese**, freshly grated

Spray a 20 x 30 cm (8 x 12 inch) baking dish lightly
with spray oil. Cut the aubergines into thin slices,
brush the slices with the oil and season with a little
salt and pepper. Cook under a preheated high grill for
2–3 minutes on each side until charred and softened.

Layer the aubergine slices, tomato sauce and
mozzarella in the prepared baking dish to give 3 layers
of each, ending with the mozzarella. Scatter over the
Parmesan.

Bake in a preheated oven, 200°C (400°F), Gas Mark
6, for 20–25 minutes until bubbling and golden. Serve
with a crisp green salad and some crusty bread.

For aubergine & mozzarella cannelloni, prepare the
aubergines and cook under a grill as above. Cut the
mozzarella into cubes and roll each slice of aubergine
up with a cube of mozzarella and a basil leaf inside to
form the cannelloni. Place in the oiled baking dish,
pour over the tomato sauce and scatter over an extra
75 g (3 oz) grated mozzarella and the grated
Parmesan. Bake as above.

mixed vegetable curry

Serves **4** as a main dish or
6 as a side dish
Preparation time **15 minutes**
Cooking time **20–30 minutes**

2–3 tablespoons **vegetable oil**
1 small **onion**, chopped, or
2 teaspoons **cumin seeds**
500 g (1 lb) **mixed vegetables**, such as potatoes, carrots, swede, peas, French beans and cauliflower, cut into chunks or broken into florets (French beans can be left whole)
about 1 teaspoon **chilli powder**
2 teaspoons **ground coriander**
½ teaspoon **ground turmeric**
2–3 **tomatoes**, skinned and chopped, or **juice** of 1 **lemon**
300 ml (½ pint) **water** (optional)
salt

Heat the oil in a heavy-based saucepan, add the onion and cook over a medium heat, stirring occasionally, for about 10 minutes, or until golden. Alternatively, add the cumin seeds and cook, stirring frequently, until they sizzle.

Add the vegetables, chilli powder, coriander, turmeric and salt to taste and cook, stirring constantly, for 2–3 minutes.

Stir in the tomatoes or the lemon juice. If a dry vegetable curry is preferred, add only a little water, cover and cook gently for 10–12 minutes until dry. For a more moist curry, stir in the measurement water, cover and simmer for 5–6 minutes until the vegetables are tender.

Serve as a main dish with naan, chappatis or basmati rice, or on its own as a side dish.

For buttery spiced pitta bread to serve as an accompaniment, lay 4 large, round pitta breads on a baking sheet and warm through in a preheated oven, 180°C (350°F), Gas Mark 4, for 10 minutes. Meanwhile, put 100 g (3½ oz) butter, 1 crushed garlic clove, ½ teaspoon ground coriander and a pinch of cayenne pepper in a saucepan and cook gently for 3–4 minutes until the garlic is soft and golden. Remove the pitta bread from the oven and brush the spiced butter mixture all over each one.

chickpea tagine

Serves **4**

Preparation time **15 minutes**

Cooking time **40 minutes**

100 ml (3½ fl oz) **extra virgin olive oil**

1 large **onion**, finely chopped

2 **garlic cloves**, crushed

2 teaspoons **ground coriander**

1 teaspoon each **ground cumin, ground turmeric** and **ground cinnamon**

1 large **aubergine**, about 375 g (12 oz), diced

400 g (13 oz) can **chickpeas**, drained

400 g (13 oz) can chopped **tomatoes**

300 ml (½ pint) **vegetable stock** (see page 58 for homemade)

250 g (8 oz) **button mushrooms**

75 g (3 oz) **dried figs**, chopped

2 tablespoons chopped **fresh coriander**

salt and **black pepper**

preserved lemon, chopped, to serve

Heat 2 tablespoons of the oil in a saucepan, add the onion, garlic and spices and cook over a medium heat, stirring frequently, for 5 minutes until lightly golden.

Heat a further 2 tablespoons of the oil in the pan, add the aubergines and cook, stirring, for 4–5 minutes until browned. Add the chickpeas, tomatoes and stock and bring to the boil. Reduce the heat, cover and simmer gently for 20 minutes.

Meanwhile, heat the remaining oil in a frying pan, add the mushrooms and cook over a medium heat for 4–5 minutes until browned.

Add the mushrooms to the tagine with the figs and cook for a further 10 minutes. Stir in the coriander. Garnish with chopped preserved lemon and serve with couscous (see below).

For buttered couscous to serve as an accompaniment, put 250 g (8 oz) couscous in a heatproof bowl and pour over 250 ml (8 fl oz) boiling vegetable stock. Cover the bowl with a clean tea towel and leave to stand for 5 minutes, or until the grains are swollen and all the liquid has been absorbed. Add 50 g (2 oz) diced softened butter and gently fork through the grains to separate.

ratatouille

Serves **8**
Preparation time **10 minutes**
Cooking time **30 minutes**

125 ml (4 fl oz) **olive oil**
2 large **aubergines**, quartered
    lengthways and cut into
    1 cm (½ inch) slices
2 **courgettes**, cut into 1 cm
    (½ inch) slices
2 large **red peppers**, cored,
    deseeded and cut into
    squares
1 large **yellow pepper**, cored,
    deseeded and cut into
    squares
2 large **onions**, thinly sliced
3 large **garlic cloves**, crushed
2 tablespoons **tomato purée**
400 g (13 oz) can **plum
    tomatoes**
12 **basil leaves**, chopped
1 tablespoon finely chopped
    marjoram or **oregano**
1 teaspoon finely chopped
    thyme
1 tablespoon **paprika**
2–4 tablespoons finely
    chopped **parsley**
salt and **black pepper**

Heat half the oil in a roasting tin in a preheated oven, 220°C (425°F), Gas Mark 7. Add the aubergines, courgettes and peppers and toss in the hot oil. Return to the oven and roast for about 30 minutes, or until tender.

Meanwhile, heat the remaining oil in a deep saucepan, add the onions and garlic and cook over a medium heat for 3–5 minutes until softened but not browned. Add the tomato purée, plum tomatoes, herbs and paprika and season to taste with salt and pepper. Stir to combine, then cook for 10–15 minutes until the mixture is thick and syrupy.

Using a slotted spoon, transfer the vegetables from the roasting tin to the tomato mixture. Gently stir to combine, then add the parsley and adjust seasoning if necessary. Serve hot or cold with crusty bread or as an accompaniment to meats or poultry.

For ratatouille tartlets, using a 7 cm (3 inch) pastry cutter, stamp out 16 rounds from each of 2 x 30 cm (12 inch) sheets of thawed frozen shortcrust pastry. Press into 2 patty pans. Prick the bases with a fork and chill in the refrigerator for 30 minutes. Meanwhile, prepare the ratatouille as above, but make only half the quantity. Bake the cases in a preheated oven, 200°C (400°F), Gas Mark 6, for 10–12 minutes until golden. Spoon a little of the hot ratatouille into each case, scatter with 25 g (1 oz) grated Parmesan cheese and serve as an appetizer.

halloumi & fig pastry pizza

Serves **2**
Preparation time **10 minutes**
Cooking time **25 minutes**

1 sheet of **frozen puff pastry**,
   25 cm (10 inches) square,
   thawed
3 tablespoons **green pesto**
   (see page 128 for
   homemade)
4 **fresh figs**, quartered
200 g (7 oz) **halloumi
   cheese**, thinly sliced
50 g (2 oz) **pitted black
   olives**, halved
2 tablespoons freshly grated
   Parmesan cheese
a few **mint leaves**, to garnish
salt and **black pepper**

Lay the pastry on a baking sheet and score a 1 cm
(½ inch) border around the edge. Prick the base with
a fork and spread the centre with the pesto.

Arrange the figs, halloumi and olives over the pesto
and scatter over the Parmesan.

Place the baking sheet on another preheated baking
sheet (this will ensure the pastry is crispy) and bake
in a preheated oven, 200°C (400°F), Gas Mark 6, for
10 minutes. Reduce the temperature to 160°C (325°F),
Gas Mark 3, and bake for a further 15 minutes until
the base is crispy. Scatter the mint leaves over to
garnish and serve with a rocket salad.

For mini puff pastries, use a 5 cm (2 inch) pastry
cutter to stamp out rounds from the pastry sheet.
Top each with a spoonful of olive tapenade and a slice
of fresh fig, then divide 150 g (5 oz) crumbled goats'
cheese between the rounds. Scatter over the
Parmesan and bake as above for 8–10 minutes.
Serve warm.

layered cheese & tomato soufflé

Serves **4**
Preparation time **15 minutes**, plus cooling
Cooking time **45–50 minutes**

25 g (1 oz) **butter**, plus extra for greasing
1 **garlic clove**, crushed
1 small **onion**, chopped
375 g (12 oz) **tomatoes**, skinned and chopped
2 teaspoons **dried oregano**
6–8 **pitted black olives**, chopped
salt and **black pepper**

Soufflé mixture
40 g (1½ oz) **butter**
40 g (1½ oz) **plain flour**
300 ml (½ pint) **single cream** or **milk**
3 large **eggs**, separated
150 g (5 oz) **full-fat soft cheese with garlic and herbs**, crumbled

Melt the butter in a heavy-based saucepan, add the garlic, onion and tomatoes and cook over a low heat, stirring occasionally, for 3–4 minutes. Add the oregano and olives and season to taste with salt and pepper. Remove the pan from the heat and leave to cool.

Meanwhile, for the soufflé, melt the butter in a saucepan, add the flour and cook, stirring constantly, for 1 minute. Remove the pan from the heat and gradually add the cream or milk, stirring vigorously after each addition to ensure that it is fully incorporated. Return the pan to the heat and bring to the boil, stirring constantly, until thickened. Remove from the heat and beat in the egg yolks, 1 at a time. Add the cheese and stir until it has completely melted. Remove from the heat and leave to cool.

Whisk the egg whites in a large bowl until just stiff enough to stand in peaks. Mix about 2 tablespoons of the egg whites into the cheese mixture, then carefully fold in the remaining egg whites with a metal spoon.

Grease a 1.5 litre (2½ pint) soufflé dish and place it on a baking sheet. Spread the cooled tomato mixture in the dish and cover with the soufflé mixture. Bake immediately in a preheated oven, 190°C (375°F), Gas Mark 5, for 35–40 minutes until well risen and golden brown. Serve immediately.

cheese & spinach tart

Serves **4**
Preparation time **10 minutes**
Cooking time **25 minutes**

50 g (2 oz) **butter**
1 small **onion**, finely
 chopped
1 **garlic clove**, crushed
2 teaspoons chopped **thyme**
250 g (8 oz) **frozen leaf
 spinach**, thawed
175 ml (6 fl oz) **single cream**
2 **eggs**, beaten
25 g (1 oz) **Parmesan
 cheese**, freshly grated
20 cm (8 inch) **frozen pastry
 tart case** (cook from
 frozen)
salt and **black pepper**

Melt the butter in a large frying pan, add the onion, garlic, thyme and salt and pepper to taste and cook for 5 minutes. Squeeze out all the excess water from the spinach, add to the pan and cook, stirring, for 2–3 minutes until heated through.

Beat together the cream, eggs, cheese and a pinch of salt and pepper in a bowl. Spoon the spinach mixture into the tart case, carefully pour over the cream mixture and bake on a preheated baking sheet in a preheated oven, 200°C (400°F), Gas Mark 6, for 20 minutes until set. Serve with a green salad.

For mushroom & soured cream tart, cook the onion, garlic and thyme in the butter as above, then add 375 g (12 oz) halved button mushrooms to the pan and cook until browned. Omit the spinach and continue as above, but replace the single cream with 175 ml (6 fl oz) soured cream.

baked cheese fondue

Serves **4**
Preparation time **5 minutes**
Cooking time **12–15 minutes**

1 whole **Camembert cheese**,
  about 200 g (7 oz)
1 tablespoon **extra virgin
  olive oil**
1 tablespoon **clear honey**
2 teaspoons chopped **thyme
  leaves**, plus a few extra to
  garnish
1 **baguette**, sliced
250 g (8 oz) **vine cherry
  tomatoes**
1 **dessert apple** or **pear**, cut
  into wedges
salt and **black pepper**

Put the Camembert on a baking sheet lined with foil.
Drizzle over the oil and honey and scatter over the
thyme and salt and pepper to taste.

Bake in a preheated oven, 200°C (400°F), Gas Mark
6, for 12–15 minutes until the cheese is sizzling and
ready to burst through the skin.

Carefully transfer to a platter and serve with the bread,
tomatoes and fruit to dip into the oozing cheese.

For a fruit & nut baked cheese fondue, prepare and
bake the cheese as above, then top with 2 quartered
fresh figs and 2 tablespoons toasted and roughly
chopped pecan nuts.

cheesy pasta & mushroom bake

Serves **4**
Preparation time **10 minutes**
Cooking time **35–40 minutes**

spray olive oil, for oiling
3 tablespoons **extra virgin olive oil**
1 **onion**, finely chopped
2 **garlic cloves**, crushed
2 teaspoons chopped **sage**
250 g (8 oz) **button mushrooms**, quartered
500 g (1 lb) **cheese sauce** (see below for homemade)
375 g (12 oz) **dried penne**
2 tablespoons chopped **parsley**
4 tablespoons freshly grated **Parmesan cheese**
salt and **black pepper**

Spray 4 x 300 ml (½ pint) baking dishes lightly with spray oil. Heat 1 tablespoon of the olive oil in a frying pan, add the onion, garlic, sage and salt and pepper to taste and cook gently for 10 minutes until softened. Add the remaining oil, then increase the heat to high, add the mushrooms and cook, stirring, for 3–4 minutes until golden.

Add the cheese sauce and heat gently for 2–3 minutes until just bubbling.

Meanwhile, plunge the pasta into a large saucepan of lightly salted boiling water. Return to the boil and cook for 10–12 minutes or until al dente. Drain well and return to the pan.

Stir the sauce into the pasta with the parsley and season to taste with salt and pepper.

Spoon the pasta into the prepared dish and scatter over the Parmesan. Bake in a preheated oven, 190°C (375°F), Gas Mark 5, for 15–20 minutes until bubbling and golden. Serve with a crisp green salad.

For homemade cheese sauce, melt 50 g (2 oz) unsalted butter in a saucepan and stir in 50 g (2 oz) plain flour. Cook over a low heat, stirring, for 1 minute until golden. Gradually whisk in 600 ml (1 pint) milk and cook, stirring constantly, until the sauce is smooth. Bring to the boil, stirring, then reduce the heat and simmer for 2 minutes. Add salt and pepper to taste and remove the pan from the heat. Immediately stir in 100 g (3½ oz) grated Cheddar cheese.

chestnut risotto cakes

Serves **4**
Preparation time **10 minutes**,
  plus soaking
Cooking time **20 minutes**

15 g (½ oz) **dried porcini
  mushrooms**
1 tablespoon **olive oil**
175 g (6 oz) **risotto rice**
600 ml (1 pint) hot
  vegetable stock (see
  page 58 for homemade)
50 g (2 oz) **butter**
1 **onion**, chopped
3 **garlic cloves**, crushed
200 g (7 oz) **cooked peeled
  chestnuts**, chopped
75 g (3 oz) **Parmesan
  cheese**, freshly grated
1 **egg**, lightly beaten
50 g (2 oz) **polenta**
vegetable oil, for shallow-
  frying
salt and **black pepper**
lemon wedges, to garnish

Put the dried mushrooms in a heatproof bowl and cover with boiling water. Leave to soak while you prepare the rice.

Heat the olive oil in a heavy-based saucepan, add the rice and stir well to coat the grains with the oil. Add the hot stock and bring to the boil. Reduce the heat, partially cover and simmer, stirring frequently, for 12–15 minutes until the rice is tender and all the stock has been absorbed. Transfer to a bowl.

Meanwhile, melt the butter in a saucepan, add the onion and garlic and cook gently for 5 minutes.

Drain and chop the soaked mushrooms, then add to the rice with the onion mixture, chestnuts, Parmesan and egg. Stir until well combined and season to taste with salt and pepper.

Divide the mixture into 12 portions. Pat each portion into a cake and roll in the polenta. Heat a shallow depth of vegetable oil in a frying pan, add the cakes and cook for 2 minutes on each side until golden. Garnish each serving with a lemon wedge and serve immediately with mixed salad leaves.

roast vegetable & herb couscous

Serves **6**
Preparation time **15 minutes**,
  plus soaking
Cooking time **25 minutes**

500 g (1 lb) **pumpkin**,
  peeled, deseeded and
  diced
4 **courgettes**, diced
1 **red onion**, cut into wedges
75 ml (3 fl oz) **extra virgin
  olive oil**
200 g (7 oz) **couscous**
250 ml (8 fl oz) **boiling water**
250 g (8 oz) **cherry
  tomatoes**, halved
2 tablespoons each
  chopped **fresh coriander,
  mint** and **parsley**
juice of 1 large **lemon**
salt and **black pepper**

Put the pumpkin, courgettes and onion in a roasting tin with 2 tablespoons of the oil, season to taste with salt and pepper and stir to combine.

Roast in a preheated oven, 220°C (425°F), Gas Mark 7, for 25 minutes until all the vegetables are cooked.

Meanwhile, put the couscous in a heatproof bowl and pour over the measurement boiling water. Cover the bowl with a clean tea towel and leave to stand for 5 minutes, or until the grains are swollen and all the liquid has been absorbed.

Fork through the couscous to fluff up the grains, then stir in the roasted vegetables, cherry tomatoes and herbs.

Whisk together the remaining oil, the lemon juice and salt and pepper to taste in a small bowl and stir through the salad.

For vegetable kebabs with herb couscous, cut 4 courgettes into chunks and 1 red onion into wedges. Core and deseed 1 red pepper and cut into chunks. Thread the vegetables on to metal skewers, interspersed with 16 button mushrooms, brush with olive oil and season to taste with salt and pepper. Cook under a preheated high grill for 8–10 minutes, turning halfway through, until charred and cooked through. Make the couscous as above and serve with the kebabs.

bean, goats' cheese & nut salad

Serves **4**
Preparation time **10 minutes**
Cooking time **3 minutes**

500 g (1 lb) **fine green
  beans**
150 g (5 oz) **goats' cheese**,
  crumbled
100 g (3½ oz) **pecan nuts**,
  toasted
125 g (4 oz) **baby rocket
  leaves**
1 large handful **flat leaf
  parsley leaves**

Dressing
3 tablespoons **walnut oil**
1 tablespoon **extra virgin
  olive oil**
1 tablespoon **sherry vinegar**
1 teaspoon **caster sugar**
1 small **garlic clove**, crushed
salt and **black pepper**

Cook the beans in a saucepan of lightly salted boiling
water for 3 minutes.

Drain the beans well and refresh under cold water.
Drain again and pat dry. Put in a bowl with the goats'
cheese, pecan nuts, rocket and parsley.

Make the dressing. Whisk the ingredients together in
a small bowl. Add to the salad, toss well and serve.

For bean & nut salad with goats' cheese dressing,
prepare the salad as above but omit the goats' cheese.
Put 100 g (3½ oz) crumbled goats' cheese in a bowl
and whisk in 1 tablespoon raspberry wine vinegar,
2 teaspoons clear honey, 125 ml (4 fl oz) extra virgin
olive oil, 2 tablespoons boiling water and salt and
pepper to taste. Drizzle over the salad and serve.

warm lentil & goats' cheese salad

Serves **4**
Preparation time **10 minutes**
Cooking time **20–30 minutes**

2 teaspoons **olive oil**
2 teaspoons **cumin seeds**
2 **garlic cloves**, crushed
2 teaspoons grated **fresh
  root ginger**
125 g (4 oz) **Puy lentils**
750 ml (1¼ pints) **vegetable
  stock** (see page 58 for
  homemade)
2 tablespoons chopped **mint**
2 tablespoons chopped
  fresh coriander
½ **lime**
150 g (5 oz) **baby spinach
  leaves**
125 g (4 oz) **goats' cheese**,
  crumbled
black pepper

Heat the oil in a saucepan, add the cumin seeds, garlic and ginger and cook over a medium heat, stirring, for 1 minute.

Add the lentils and cook for a further minute.

Add the stock, a large ladleful at a time, and cook until each addition has been absorbed before adding the next. Continue in this way until all the stock has been absorbed. This should take about 20–30 minutes. Remove from the heat and stir in the mint and coriander with a squeeze of lime juice.

To serve, divide the spinach leaves between individual bowls, top with a quarter of the lentils and the goats' cheese and sprinkle with pepper.

For lentil salad with grilled haloumi, prepare the lentil salad as above, but omit the goats' cheese and replace the spinach leaves with 150 g (5 oz) rocket leaves. Cut 250 g (8 oz) haloumi cheese into 8 slices. Heat a nonstick frying pan until hot, add the cheese slices and cook over a high heat for 1 minute on each side until charred and softened. Arrange the haloumi slices over the salad, squeeze over the juice from ½ lemon and drizzle over a little extra virgin olive oil.

roasted sweet potato salad

Serves **4**

Preparation time **15 minutes**, plus cooling

Cooking time **30–35 minutes**

500 g (1 lb) **sweet potatoes**, peeled and cubed

2 tablespoons **extra virgin olive oil**

1 teaspoon **ground coriander**

½ teaspoon **ground cumin**

¼ teaspoon **ground cinnamon**

175 g (6 oz) **green beans**

150 g (5 oz) **baby spinach leaves**

50 g (2 oz) **shelled pistachio nuts**, toasted

salt and **black pepper**

Dressing

2 tablespoons **natural yogurt**

1 small **garlic clove**, crushed

1 large **red chilli**, deseeded and finely chopped

1 tablespoon **lemon juice**

1 teaspoon **clear honey**

50 ml (2 fl oz) **extra virgin olive oil**

Put the sweet potatoes in a roasting tin. Combine the oil, spices and salt and pepper to taste in a small bowl, pour over the potatoes and stir well to evenly coat.

Roast in a preheated oven, 220°C (425°F), Gas Mark 7, for 30–35 minutes, stirring halfway through, until golden and tender. Leave to cool for 30 minutes.

Meanwhile, blanch the beans in a saucepan of lightly salted boiling water for 2–3 minutes until just tender. Drain and refresh under cold water. Drain again and pat dry.

Put the beans in a large bowl with the cooled sweet potatoes, spinach leaves and pistachio nuts.

Make the dressing. Mix together the yogurt, garlic, chilli, lemon juice, honey and salt and pepper to taste in a bowl. Whisk in the oil until evenly blended. Pour over the salad, stir well and serve.

For sesame and soy dressing as an alternative for the salad, whisk together 2 tablespoons olive oil, 2 teaspoons sesame oil, 1 tablespoon light soy sauce, 1 teaspoon clear honey and a little pepper in a small bowl. Prepare the salad as above and serve drizzled with the dressing, garnished with 2 tablespoons toasted sesame seeds.

easy puds
& cakes

lemon creams with raspberries

Serves **4**
Preparation time **5 minutes**,
   plus chilling & standing
Cooking time **5 minutes**

400 ml (14 fl oz) **double
   cream**
100 g (3½ oz) **caster sugar**
100 ml (3½ fl oz) **lemon juice**
150 g (5 oz) **fresh
   raspberries**
2 tablespoons **icing sugar**

Heat the cream and caster sugar together in a saucepan until the sugar has dissolved. Bring to the boil, then reduce the heat and simmer for 3 minutes.

Remove the pan from the heat, add the lemon juice and immediately pour into 4 x 150 ml (¼ pint) ramekins. Set aside to cool completely, then chill overnight in the refrigerator.

Combine the raspberries and icing sugar in a bowl and mash lightly. Leave to stand for 30 minutes until really juicy. Spoon the raspberry mixture on to the lemon creams and serve with crispy cinnamon cookies (see below).

For crispy cinnamon cookies to serve as an accompaniment, spray 2 baking sheets lightly with spray olive oil. Put 250 g (8 oz) softened unsalted butter, 125 g (4 oz) caster sugar, 1 tablespoon milk, 300 g (10 oz) self-raising flour and 1 teaspoon ground cinnamon in a food processor and process until smooth. Roll small pieces of the dough into balls and flatten into 5 cm (2 inch) discs. Place on the prepared baking sheets and bake in a preheated oven, 180°C (350°F), Gas Mark 4, for 12–15 minutes until lightly golden. Leave to cool on the baking sheets for 5 minutes, then transfer to a wire rack to cool completely.

sticky toffee puddings

Serves **4**
Preparation time **10 minutes**
Cooking time **25–30 minutes**

spray olive oil, for oiling
2 tablespoons **golden syrup**
2 tablespoons **black treacle**
150 g (5 oz) **butter**, softened
2 tablespoons **double cream**
125 g (4 oz) **caster sugar**
2 **eggs**, beaten
100 g (3½ oz) **self-raising flour**
50 g (2 oz) **walnuts**, lightly toasted and ground

Spray 4 x 200 ml (7 fl oz) ramekins lightly with spray oil. In a small saucepan, heat together the golden syrup, treacle and 50 g (2 oz) of the butter until melted. Divide half the mixture between the prepared ramekins, stir double cream into the remainder and set aside.

Put the remaining butter and sugar in a food processor and process briefly. Add the eggs and flour and process again for 30 seconds. Stir in the walnuts.

Spoon the sponge mixture into the ramekins to cover the syrup mixture.

Stand the ramekins in a shallow roasting tin and bake in a preheated oven, 180°C (350°F), Gas Mark 4, for 25–30 minutes until risen and golden.

Remove the ramekins from the oven and leave to stand for 5 minutes. Meanwhile, heat the remaining treacle mixture. Unmould the puddings and pour over the treacle. Serve with custard (see page 218 for homemade) or clotted cream.

For sticky date & orange puddings, prepare the golden syrup mixture, dividing half the mixture between ramekins and stirring cream into the remainder as above. Process the remaining butter and sugar, then add the eggs and flour as above. Fold in 125 g (4 oz) finely chopped dates, grated zest of 1 orange and 25 g (1 oz) ground pecan nuts. Spoon over the syrup mixture and bake as above. Serve with the warmed treacle as above.

summer pudding

Serves **8**

Preparation time **15 minutes**, plus chilling

Cooking time **10–15 minutes**

250 g (8 oz) **fresh** or **frozen redcurrants**, thawed if frozen, plus extra sprigs to decorate (optional)

125 g (4 oz) **caster sugar**

250 g (8 oz) **fresh** or **frozen strawberries**, thawed if frozen

250 g (8 oz) **fresh** or **frozen raspberries**, thawed if frozen

8 slices of **white bread**, crusts removed

Put the redcurrants and sugar in a heavy-based saucepan and cook over a low heat, stirring occasionally, for 10–15 minutes until tender. Add the strawberries and raspberries, remove from the heat and leave to cool. Strain the fruit, reserving the juice.

Cut 3 rounds of bread the same diameter as a 900 ml (1½ pint) pudding basin. Shape the remaining bread to fit around the side of the basin. Soak all the bread in the reserved fruit juice.

Line the base of the basin with one of the rounds, then arrange the shaped bread around the side. Pour in half the fruit and place another round of bread on top. Cover with the remaining fruit, then top with the remaining bread round.

Cover with a saucer small enough to fit inside the basin and put a 500 g (1 lb) weight on top. Chill in the refrigerator overnight.

Turn out on to a serving plate, pour over any remaining fruit juice and decorate with a few reducurrant sprigs arranged on top of the pudding in the centre, if wished. Serve with whipped or pouring cream.

chocolate & raspberry pudding

Serves **6**
Preparation time **15 minutes**
Cooking time **40–45 minutes**

olive oil spray, for oiling
175 g (6 oz) **fresh raspberries**
125 g (4 oz) **self-raising flour**
40 g (1½ oz) **cocoa powder**
100 g (3½ oz) **caster sugar**
250 ml (8 fl oz) **milk**
75 g (3 oz) **unsalted butter**, melted
2 **eggs**, beaten

Topping
75 g (3 oz) **caster sugar**
75 g (3 oz) **soft light brown sugar**
2 tablespoons **cocoa powder**
350 ml (12 fl oz) **boiling water**
icing sugar, for dusting

Spray a 1 litre (1¾ pint) baking dish lightly with spray oil. Scatter the raspberries over the base of the dish.

Sift the flour and cocoa powder into a bowl and stir in the caster sugar. Make a well in the centre and whisk in the milk, melted butter and eggs to form a smooth batter (it should be quite runny). Pour the mixture into the dish, covering the raspberries.

Make the topping. Combine the sugars and cocoa powder and sprinkle over the top of the chocolate mixture. Very carefully pour the measurement boiling water over the top as evenly as possible.

Bake in a preheated oven, 180°C (350°F), Gas Mark 4, for 40–45 minutes until the pudding is firm to the touch and some 'bubbles' of sauce appear on the top. Rest for 5 minutes, then dust with icing sugar and serve.

For chocolate & orange pudding, make the chocolate pudding mixture as above, but omit the raspberries. Pour the mixture into the baking dish. For the topping, combine the sugars and cocoa powder and sprinkle over the pudding mixture as above. Pour 350 ml (12 fl oz) orange juice into a saucepan and heat until boiling point. Stir in 2 tablespoons of Cointreau or brandy. Pour over the top of the pudding mixture. Bake in the oven as above, dust with icing sugar and serve with whipped cream.

venetian rice pudding

Serves **4**
Preparation time **10 minutes**,
  plus soaking
Cooking time **20–30 minutes**

75 g (3 oz) **sultanas**
3 tablespoons **medium sherry**
  (optional)
600 ml (1 pint) hot **semi-
  skimmed milk**
150 ml (¼ pint) **double cream**
1 **vanilla pod**, split
  lengthways, or 2 teaspoons
  vanilla extract
50 g (2 oz) **caster sugar**
½ teaspoon **ground mixed
  spice**
grated **rind** of 1 **lemon**
125 g (4 oz) **risotto rice**
strips of **lemon rind**, to
  decorate

Put the sultanas in a bowl with the sherry, if using,
and leave to soak while you prepare the risotto.

Put milk, cream, vanilla pod or extract, sugar, mixed
spice and grated lemon rind in a saucepan and bring
almost to the boil.

Add the rice to the pan and cook on the lowest heat,
stirring frequently, for 20–30 minutes, or until the rice
is creamy but the grains are still firm.

Stir in the sultanas and any sherry from the bowl and
serve warm or cold, decorated with lemon rind strips.

For coconut rice pudding with mango, put 150 g
(5 oz) short-grain rice, 1 litre (1¾ pints) coconut milk
and 50 g (2 oz) caster sugar in a saucepan. Bring to
the boil, then reduce the heat and cook gently, stirring
occasionally, for 25–30 minutes until the milk has
been absorbed and the rice is tender. Spoon into
bowls and serve topped with 1 peeled, stoned and
sliced mango and a drizzle of clear honey.

muesli berry crumble

Serves **4**
Preparation time **10 minutes**
Cooking time **20 minutes**

spray olive oil, for oiling
150 g (5 oz) **fresh blueberries**
150 g (5 oz) **fresh strawberries**, hulled and halved
2 **peaches**, quartered, stoned and sliced
4 tablespoons **orange juice**
2 tablespoons **soft light brown sugar**
25 g (1 oz) **butter**, diced
250 g (8 oz) **good-quality muesli**
1 tablespoon **plain flour**
4 tablespoons **single cream**, plus extra to serve

Spray 4 x 250 ml (8 fl oz) ramekins lightly with spray oil. Combine the berries, peaches, orange juice and sugar in a bowl, then divide between the prepared ramekins. Add half the butter to the ramekins.

Put the muesli in a bowl, add the flour and cream and stir until all the muesli is moistened. Sprinkle over the top of the fruit mixture in the ramekins and add the remaining butter.

Stand the ramekins in a shallow roasting tin and bake in a preheated oven, 180°C (350°F), Gas Mark 4, for 20 minutes until the topping is golden and the fruit bubbling. Serve with cream.

For apple & blackberry crumble, put 500 g (1 lb) peeled and diced apples and 125 g (4 oz) fresh or frozen blackberries in a saucepan with 2 tablespoons caster sugar, 25 g (1 oz) butter, 1 teaspoon ground cinnamon and 4 tablespoons water. Warm through for 5 minutes until the butter is melted and the fruit softened. Divide between the oiled ramekins, add the muesli topping and bake as above. Serve with custard (see page 218 for homemade).

freeform apple tart

Serves **6**
Preparation time **10 minutes**
Cooking time **20–25 minutes**

1 large sheet of **shortcrust
pastry**, 30 cm (12 inch)
square, thawed if frozen
500 g (1 lb) **Granny Smith
apples**, peeled, cored and
thinly sliced
50 g (2 oz) **raisins**
25 g (1 oz) **soft light brown
sugar**
25 g (1 oz) **butter**, melted
½ teaspoon **ground
cinnamon**
1 tablespoon **milk**
1 tablespoon **icing sugar**,
plus extra to serve

Lay the pastry sheet on a baking sheet lined with
baking paper and trim each corner to make a roughly
round piece of pastry.

Mix together the apples, raisins, brown sugar, melted
butter and cinnamon in a bowl until evenly combined.
Spoon the apple mixture on to the pastry sheet,
arranging it in a circle, leaving a 2.5 cm (1 inch) border.
Pull the pastry edges up and over the filling to make a
rim. Brush the pastry with the milk and dust with the
icing sugar.

Bake in a preheated oven, 180°C (350°F), Gas Mark 4,
for 20–25 minutes until the pastry is golden and the
fruit softened. Dust with extra icing sugar and serve
warm with custard (see below).

For homemade custard to serve as an accompaniment,
put 600 ml (1 pint) milk and 1 vanilla pod, split
lengthways, in a saucepan and heat gently until it
reaches boiling point. Remove from the heat and leave
to infuse for 15 minutes. Remove the vanilla pod.
Whisk 6 egg yolks and 2 tablespoons caster sugar
together in a bowl until pale and creamy, then stir in
the infused milk. Return to the pan and cook, stirring
constantly, until the mixture thickens enough to coat the
back of the spoon Do not let the custard boil, or it will
curdle. Serve hot.

bread & butter pudding

Serves **4**
Preparation time **15 minutes**,
  plus standing
Cooking time **30–40 minutes**

4 thin slices of **day-old white
  bread**
50 g (2 oz) **unsalted butter**,
  plus extra for greasing
50 g (2 oz) **sultanas**
25 g (1 oz) **mixed peel**
  (optional)
grated **rind** of 1 **lemon**
300 ml (½ pint) **single cream**
  and 300 ml (½ pint) **milk** or
  600 ml (1 pint) **milk**
2 **eggs**, plus 2 **egg yolks**
25 g (1 oz) **granulated sugar**
½ teaspoon freshly grated
  nutmeg
1–2 tablespoons **jelly
  marmalade**, heated

Spread the bread slices with the butter and cut each into 4 triangles. Place a layer of bread in the base of a greased 1 litre (1¾ pint) pie dish. Sprinkle the sultanas, mixed peel, if using, and lemon rind over the top and cover with the remaining bread triangles.

Beat the cream, if using, with the milk, eggs, egg yolks and sugar in a bowl. Pour the mixture over the bread. Cover and leave to stand for 30 minutes.

Sprinkle the nutmeg over the surface and bake in a preheated oven, 180°C (350°F), Gas Mark 4, for 30–40 minutes.

Remove from the oven and brush the hot marmalade over the top. Serve hot, with cream or stewed fruit, if liked.

For stewed summer berries to serve with the pudding, put 500 g (1 lb) mixed summer berries, such as blackberries, blackcurrants and raspberries, 50 g (2 oz) caster sugar, pared rind and juice of ½ lemon and ¼ teaspoon ground allspice in a large saucepan. Heat gently until the sugar has dissolved, then simmer over a very low heat for 5–10 minutes until the fruits are softened and juicy.

tiramisu with white chocolate

Serves **4**

Preparation time **10 minutes**,
plus chilling

100 ml (3½ fl oz) freshly
made **black coffee**, cooled

3 tablespoons **Frangelico**

100 g (3½ oz) shop-bought
sponge cake

450 ml (¾ pint) **double
cream**

2 tablespoons **icing sugar**

3 **egg whites**

50 g (2 oz) **white chocolate**,
grated

Combine the coffee and Frangelico. Cut the sponge cake into cubes and divide half the cubes between 4 glasses. Add a tablespoon of the coffee mixture to each glass.

Whip the cream with the sugar and half the remaining coffee mixture in a bowl until soft peaks form.

Whisk the egg whites in a separate bowl until stiff, then carefully fold into the cream mixture.

Spoon half the cream mixture into the glasses and top with the remaining sponge cubes, coffee mixture and cream mixture. Sprinkle with the chocolate. Chill in the refrigerator for 1 hour.

For raspberry & dark chocolate tiramisu, combine the coffee as above with 3 tablespoons kirsch. Divide the sponge cake cubes between 4 glasses, then add a tablespoon of the coffee mixture and a few fresh raspberries to each. Make the cream mixture and assemble the desserts as above. Add 3 more raspberries to each, then sprinkle over 50 g (2 oz) grated plain dark chocolate.

fruit salad with elderflower syrup

Serves **4**
Preparation time **5 minutes**,
  plus cooling & standing
Cooking time **5 minutes**

150 ml (¼ pint) **orange juice**
50 ml (2 fl oz) **elderflower
  syrup**
1 **vanilla pod**, split lengthways
200 g (7 oz) **fresh
  blueberries**
200 g (5 oz) **fresh
  strawberries**, hulled and
  halved
200 g (5 oz) **fresh
  raspberries**
150 g (5 oz) **seedless grapes**
2 **oranges**, segmented

Combine the orange juice, elderflower syrup and vanilla pod in a saucepan and heat gently until just boiling. Reduce the heat and simmer gently for 5 minutes. Remove the pan from the heat and leave to cool for 30 minutes.

Put all the fruits in a bowl and mix together gently. Add the syrup mixture and leave to stand for 15 minutes. Serve in bowls with shortbread biscuits.

For rosewater & honey fruit salad, place 3 tablespoons clear honey, 150 ml (¼ pint) cold water and 1–2 tablespoons rosewater in a saucepan and heat gently until just boiling. Reduce the heat and simmer gently for 5 minutes. Remove the pan from the heat and leave to cool for 30 minutes. Pour over the combined fruits as above and serve decorated with rose petals.

bananas en papillote

Serves **4**

Preparation time
2–3 minutes

Cooking time **3–4 minutes**

butter, for greasing
4 small firm **bananas**
1 **cinnamon stick**, cut into
  quarters
4 **star anise**
1 **vanilla pod**, cut into
  quarters
2 tablespoons **grated carob**
75 ml (3 fl oz) **pineapple
  juice**

Lightly grease 4 pieces of foil or greaseproof paper, each large enough to wrap a banana. Put a banana in the centre and add a piece of cinnamon stick, 1 star anise and a piece of vanilla pod.

Sprinkle each with a quarter of the carob and pineapple juice. Seal the edges of the foil or paper together to form parcels.

Transfer the parcels to a baking sheet and bake in a preheated oven, 230°C (450°F), Gas Mark 8, for 3–4 minutes. Alternatively, cook on top of a preheated barbecue or by the side of a bonfire – in both cases, use double-thickness foil to prevent splits and spillages. Serve with crème fraîche or mascarpone cheese.

For bananas with toffee & pecan sauce, heat 75 g (3 oz) unsalted butter, 75 ml (3 fl oz) maple syrup and 75 ml (3 fl oz) double cream in a saucepan over a low heat until the butter has melted. Increase the heat and simmer briskly for 5 minutes until the sauce has thickened. Stir in 75 g (3 oz) chopped toasted pecan nuts and simmer for a further 1 minute. Set aside to cool for 15–20 minutes. Serve the sauce warm drizzled over 4 peeled and sliced ripe bananas, or over bananas cooked with the spices as above.

caramel ice cream cake

Serves **8–10**

Preparation time **10 minutes**, plus standing, chilling & freezing

1 litre (1¾ pints) **good-quality vanilla ice cream**
250 g (8 oz) **digestive biscuits**, crushed
75 g (3 oz) **butter**, melted
200 g (7 oz) **soft butterscotch fudge**
2 tablespoons **single cream**

Remove the ice cream from the freezer and leave to stand at room temperature for 30–45 minutes until it is well softened.

Meanwhile, put the crushed biscuits in a bowl, add the melted butter and mix together until the biscuits are moistened. Press the biscuit mixture into a 23 cm (9 inch) round springform tin, pressing it up the edge of the tin to give a 2.5 cm (1 inch) side. Chill in the refrigerator for 20 minutes.

Put the fudge and cream in a saucepan and heat gently, stirring, until the fudge has melted. Carefully spread two-thirds of the fudge mixture over the biscuit case. Spoon the ice cream over the top and level the surface.

Drizzle the remaining caramel over the ice cream with a spoon and freeze for 4 hours. Unmould the cake and serve in wedges.

For a chocolate & caramel cake, make the biscuit case as above, but use 250 g (8 oz) crushed chocolate digestive biscuits or chocolate cookies. Melt the fudge with the cream as above, then stir in 125 g (4 oz) toasted ground hazelnuts. Pour all the mixture into the biscuit base, then top with the softened vanilla ice cream. Melt 50 g (2 oz) plain dark chocolate in a heatproof bowl set over a saucepan of gently simmering water (don't let the bowl touch the water). Drizzle over the ice cream and freeze as above.

nectarine brûlée

Serves **6**
Preparation time **10 minutes**
Cooking time **10–15 minutes**

500 g (1 lb) **nectarines,**
  stoned and sliced
4 tablespoons **orange**
  liqueur, plus extra to
  flavour the fruit
350 ml (12 fl oz) **soured**
  cream
pinch of freshly grated
  nutmeg
1 teaspoon **vanilla extract**
125 g (4 oz) **soft light brown**
  sugar

Put the nectarines in a saucepan and add enough water to cover. Poach over a low heat for 5–10 minutes, or until tender. Drain and divide between 6 individual ramekins. Stir in a little orange liqueur.

Beat together the soured cream, nutmeg, vanilla extract and the 4 tablespoons orange liqueur in a bowl until well combined. Spoon over the nectarine slices, then scatter the sugar over the top in a thick layer.

Cook under a preheated high grill until the sugar caramelizes. Serve with brandy snaps, langues du chat or amaretti.

For lemon cookies to serve with the brûlée, put 125 g (4 oz) softened butter, 50 g (2 oz) caster sugar, grated rind of 1 lemon and ½ tablespoon lemon juice in a bowl. Using an electric hand-held whisk, beat together until pale and light. Sift in 150 g (5 oz) self-raising flour and continue beating to form a stiff dough. Take walnut-sized pieces of the dough, roll into balls and flatten into 5 cm (2 inch) discs. Place on a large baking sheet lined with baking paper and bake in a preheated oven, 180°C (350°F), Gas Mark 4, for 12–15 minutes until lightly golden. Leave to cool on the baking sheet for 5 minutes, then transfer to a wire rack to cool completely.

easy chocolate fudge cake

Makes **12 portions**
Preparation time **10 minutes**
Cooking time **50–55 minutes**

250 g (8 oz) **plain dark chocolate**, broken into pieces
250 g (8 oz) **butter**, plus extra for greasing
4 **eggs**, beaten
125 g (4 oz) **caster sugar**
225 g (7½ oz) **self-raising flour**, sifted

Icing
175 g (6 oz) **plain dark chocolate**, broken into pieces
150 ml (¼ pint) **single cream**

Grease a 20 x 30 cm (8 x 12 inch) baking tin and line the base with baking paper. Put the chocolate and butter in a heatproof bowl set over a saucepan of gently simmering water (don't let the bowl touch the water) and stir over a low heat until melted. Leave to cool for 5 minutes.

Meanwhile, using an electric hand-held whisk, whisk together the eggs and sugar in a bowl for 5 minutes until thick. Beat in the cooled chocolate mixture and fold in the flour.

Spoon the mixture into the prepared tin and bake in a preheated oven, 160°C (325°F), Gas Mark 3, for 45–50 minutes until risen and firm to the touch. Leave to cool in the tin for 10 minutes, then turn out on to a wire rack to cool completely, removing the paper from the base.

Meanwhile, make the icing. Put the chocolate in a saucepan with the cream and heat gently, stirring, until the chocolate has melted. Leave to cool for 1 hour until thickened to a pouring consistency, then spread over the cake. Leave to set for 30 minutes before serving.

For chocolate butter icing, instead of the cream icing, beat together 200 g (7 oz) softened butter, 200 g (7 oz) icing sugar and 50 g (2 oz) sifted cocoa powder in a bowl until evenly combined. Spread over the cake and serve topped with 50 g (2 oz) grated dark chocolate curls.

chocolate refrigerator cake

Makes **30 fingers**
Preparation time **15 minutes**,
    plus chilling
Cooking time **5 minutes**

500 g (1 lb) **plain dark
    chocolate**, broken into
    pieces
125 g (4 oz) **unsalted butter**,
    plus extra for greasing
100 g (3½ oz) **digestive
    biscuits**, roughly crushed
100 g (3½ oz) **dried figs**,
    roughly chopped
50 g (2 oz) **dried cranberries**
50 g (2 oz) **hazelnuts**,
    toasted
50 g (2 oz) **almonds**,
    toasted and roughly
    chopped
icing sugar, for dusting
    (optional)

Grease a 17 x 23 cm (7 x 9 inch) rectangular cake tin and line the base with baking paper. Put the chocolate and butter in a heatproof bowl set over a saucepan of gently simmering water (don't let the bowl touch the water) and stir over a low heat until melted. Stir in all the remaining ingredients.

Spoon the mixture into the prepared tin. Press well into the base and sides of the tin and smooth the surface with a palette knife.

Cover with foil and chill for 4 hours or overnight in the refrigerator. Carefully work round the edges of the cake with the palette knife and unmould on to a board, removing the paper from the base. Dust with icing sugar, if wished, and serve in thin fingers.

For a white chocolate rocky road cake, put 375 g (12 oz) white chocolate, broken into pieces, in a bowl set over a saucepan of gently simmering water (don't let the bowl touch the water) and leave until melted. Meanwhile, spray a 1 kg (2 lb) loaf tin with spray olive oil and line with baking paper. Stir 200 g (7 oz) roughly chopped Turkish delight (any flavour of your choice), 75 g (3 oz) shelled pistachio nuts and 25 g (1 oz) desiccated coconut into the melted chocolate. Pour the mixture into the prepared tin, smooth the surface and refrigerate for 4 hours. Turn out, removing the paper, and cut into slices to serve.

index

pitta bread, buttery spiced 178

pizzas: halloumi & fig pastry pizza 184

tortilla pizza with salami 98

plum sauce, chicken with 114

polenta, soft 52

pork: Chinese hoisin wings 140

hoisin pork stir-fry 88

marinated pork fillet 142

mustard & tarragon pork steaks 94

pork chops baked with potatoes 42

pork chops with roasted sweet potatoes & sage 42

pork cutlets with caramel pears 70

pork fillet with Dukhah crust 142

pork spare ribs 140

roasted hoisin pork 88

sweet & sour pork noodles 114

with Savoy cabbage 146

potatoes: fish 'n' oven chips 162

perfect roast potatoes 124

pork chops baked with 42

rösti with ham & eggs 20

shepherd's pie 150

sweet potato mash 138

prawns: chilli & lemon prawns with pasta 100

curried prawn pies 166

everything rice 116

pea & prawn risotto 118

pea & prawn risotto cakes 118

prawn, cranberry & cashew nut pilaf 154

prawns, chorizo, peas & pasta 106

prawns in chillied tomato sauce 168

spicy Asian prawns with jasmine rice 100

prosciutto: asparagus & prosciutto wraps 144

pumpkin: baked pumpkin risotto 120

pumpkin soup with crispy bacon 56

pumpkin soup with olive salsa 56

roast vegetable & herb couscous 196

winter vegetable & fruit pilaf 172

quesadilla, spicy salami, mozzarella & tomato 98

raspberries: chocolate & raspberry pudding 212

lemon creams with 206

raspberry & dark chocolate tiramisu 222

white chocolate & raspberry muffins 38

ratatouille 182

ratatouille tartlets 182

red kidney beans: chilli bean & red pepper soup 66

chilli tacos 152

rice: baked pumpkin risotto 120

baked risotto with burnt butter 120

chestnut risotto cakes 194

chicken & rice bake 54

classic paella 116

coconut rice pudding with mango 214

everything rice 116

orange & mustard seed rice 146

pea & prawn risotto 118

pea & prawn risotto cakes 118

perfect rice 134

prawn, cranberry & cashew nut pilaf 154

spicy Asian prawns with jasmine rice 100

spring vegetable & herb pilaf 172

swordfish brochettes & lemon rice 154

Venetian rice pudding 214

winter vegetable & fruit pilaf 172

ricotta & mint croûtons 64

rocket: chicken, leek & rocket pasta 104

rocket & parsley pasta 164

rosewater & honey fruit salad 224

rösti: sweet potato rösti with egg & spinach 20

with ham & eggs 20

salads: Asian tuna 76

bean & nut with goats' cheese dressing 198

bean, goats' cheese & nut 198

fresh noodle 112

lamb chops with tomato, mint & feta salad 84

lentil salad with grilled haloumi 200

roast sweet potato 202

Thai beef 96

Thai tuna 76

warm lentil & goats' cheese 200

warm scallop 160

salami: spicy salami, mozzarella & tomato quesadilla 98

tortilla pizza with 98

salmon: Parma ham-wrapped 164

salmon, orange & soy parcels 82

soy & orange salmon with noodles 82

with fennel & tomatoes 156

sauces: hollandaise 32

cheese 192

custard 218

spicy tomato & olive 174

tahini 136

tangy yogurt 54

sausage meatballs, peas & pasta 106

scallops: warm scallop salad 160

with soy & honey dressing 160

sesame & soy dressing 202

sesame croûtons 64

sesame noodles 74

shepherd's pie 150

Singapore chicken noodles 110

smoked salmon scrambled eggs 18

soufflé, layered cheese & tomato 186

soups: chicken noodle 60

garlic, paprika & egg 58

gazpacho 62

pea, lettuce & lemon 64

pumpkin with crispy bacon 56

pumpkin with olive salsa 56

roasted tomato gazpacho 62

Thai chicken noodle 60

soy sauce: sesame & soy dressing 202

soy & orange salmon 82

soya beans: treacle & mustard beans 50

spaghetti: chilli & lemon prawns with pasta 100

with easy tomato sauce 174

spinach: avocado, blue cheese & spinach melt 24

cheese & spinach tart 188

acknowledgements

Executive editor: Nicola Hill
Editor: Amy Corbett
Executive art editor: Sally Bond
Designer: one2six creative limited
Photographer: Ian Wallace
Food and props stylist: Louise Pickford
Production controller: Carolin Stransky

Commissioned photography:
© Octopus Publishing Group Limited/Ian Wallace apart from the following:
© Octopus Publishing Group Limited/David Jordan 19, 156; /Gareth Sambidge 63, 77, 127, 129, 131, 133, 139, 143, 145, 147, 161, 201, 227; /Ian Wallace 23, 27; /Sean Myers 33, 67, 165; /Simon Smith 137, 169, 178, 183, 186, 211, 220, 231; /William Reavell 59, 119, 194, 214; /William Lingwood 65.